Working Morality

An introduction to moral philosophy

Peter Mullen

Edward Arnold

© Peter Mullen 1983

First published 1983
by Edward Arnold (Publishers) Ltd
41 Bedford Square, London WC1B 3DQ

Mullen, Peter
  Working with morality.
  1. Ethics
  I. Title
  170   BC55

  ISBN 0-7131-0844-4

Text set in 9/11pt IBM Baskerville by 🅰 Tek-Art, Croydon, Surrey
and printed in Great Britain by Thomson Litho Ltd, East Kilbride,
Scotland.

Working With Morality

M. Johnson.

Preface

When people talk about a general lack of moral responsibility or about a decline in standards, I think that what they are reflecting is the philosophical perplexity of our age as it affects public and private morality. This perplexity arises out of a number of historical factors: the rise of science and critical thinking; the decline of religious authority symbolised by the church; the coming into being of a multiracial society.

Against this complicated background we all still feel the need to discover the meaning of ethics. What is good? What is right? What is my duty? And none of these questions is made any simpler by the puzzling and controversial new developments in medical technology: transplants, test-tube babies, euthanasia and so on.

In a climate of uncertainty many voices compete for our attention. From some quarters we hear the call for a return to authoritarianism and old-fashioned standards; from elsewhere we have heard the pronouncements of liberal and libertarian thought. The task of the teacher is particularly difficult because he is aware of his obligation to help his pupils discover what is right but at the same time he does not want to pontificate, to moralise.

This book aims to outline the many and various grounds on which moral decisions are made. I have set out and tried to evaluate the moral philosophies of natural law and of utilitarianism and this forms the main part of the book. But it is interesting to look also at other views of morality which are prominent in our age: existentialism and Marxism. For whether the pupil is ever exposed to the direct influence of these ideas or not, he is bound to be influenced by them indirectly because of the nature of our society and the complex machinations of the mass media.

I have tried to be straightforward and analytical and to avoid being sanctimonious and moralistic. The teacher might think there are enough books of that type about already — from whatever stables they originally emerged! There are also short sections on three important moral philosophers whose work has been and continues to be influential on the way we think about morality today.

Working With Morality is the third book in a series which has included *Beginning Philosophy* and *Thinking About Religion* and it follows the pattern of those other volumes. There is, I hope, enough clear and distinct presentation of philosophical ideas and reasonable criticism of them to .

exercise the minds of young people, and sufficient ordinariness and popular reference among the 'moral cases' to prevent tedium from setting in.

I have also tried throughout to be logical and fair, since there is neither point nor virtue in being otherwise. If in the end I have concluded that morality is derived from goodwill and common sense it is because I prize these qualities above all abstract theorising and ideological solutions.

A useful reference book is *Fifty Key Words in Philosophy* by K. Ward (Lutterworth).

Peter Mullen

Contents

1 What ought we to do?

For most of the time we live our lives without giving a second thought to
how we ought to behave. This does not mean that we behave badly — only
that we conduct our lives largely by habit. Our work and leisure happens
as a matter of routine, 'in the normal course of events' as we say. It is only
when something unusual occurs that we are forced to stop and decide
what is the best thing to do. For example, suppose I am in both the school
orchestra and the swimming team. Usually the orchestra practises on
Thursdays after school and the swimming team trains on Mondays. But
one week repairs are being done to the pool on Monday, so the training
session is rearranged for Thursday, after school.

Now, what shall I do? I cannot be in two places at once. Should I go
to the training session or to the orchestra practice? I begin to think about
it. First I think, 'I much prefer swimming to scratching away on my fiddle;
I'll go to the rearranged training session.' But then I think to myself that
there is something a little suspect, a little shady, involved in doing
something just because I *prefer* to do it. Mere preference, simply liking
something, is a flimsy reason. I might, for instance, prefer to miss school
altogether on the day of the maths examination. But that *preference* does
not seem to be a good *reason* for missing school.

Perhaps my second thought is on these lines: 'Orchestra is always on
Thursdays, so I should go along to the practice as usual. It's not fair (to
the orchestra, to the music teacher, etc.) for me to miss the practice just
because the training session has been shifted to another day.'

I might try a rather more subtle form of argument with myself and with
my preferences: 'I know it's orchestra, but my swimming needs more
practice than my fiddling! So I'll go to the training session.' There are, of
course, many possible variations of this issue, many different ways of
settling it. No doubt you could think of a dozen different arguments if
you tried. The important fact about the issue is that it is a *moral issue* —
that is to say we think about it and discuss it in terms of *the right thing
to do*. I feel I am *obliged* in some way to go to the orchestra or the
swimming, that it is not simply a matter of what I would most like to do.
Of course, what I eventually do might happen to be what I would most
like to do. But that is only a coincidence. The point is that I decide on
other grounds — grounds which are not simply a case of liking or not
liking. These grounds are called *moral grounds*. I do what I believe I *ought*
to do.

Some moral problems are more serious than others. I do not suppose that the orchestra would make a mess of the end of term concert or that the swimming team would lose badly just because I missed one practice or one training session. I must decide nonetheless, even if the issue is a fairly trivial one. I deliberately picked on a trivial example to begin with to try to show that, although we are not occupied all day long with moral problems, they are not restricted to so-called 'big issues' like war and peace, abortion and euthanasia. And, by choosing a fairly trivial issue, I want to suggest that the sort of reasoning which we use to settle it is the same sort of reasoning which we use to settle the 'big issues'. They are all settled by an appeal to what I ought to do in *these* particular circumstances. They are all decided by how we define what is *good*. For, of course, what I aim to do is that which is good. Moral philosophy is the study of what is good. Its first question is 'How can I know what is good?' If we do not know what is good, then we cannot hope to do what is good. Our behaviour depends upon our knowledge.

The meaning of good

We use the word 'good' for whatever it is that is good or that we believe to be good. How do we go about discovering what 'good' means? It seems reasonable to ask first of all how we use the word 'good' in ordinary language. A good knife, for example, is one that cuts efficiently and which is not too awkward to use. A good dinner is a dinner which is nourishing and which we enjoy. A good television programme is one that informs and/or entertains us.

Here we run straight up against our first difficulty in trying to talk about 'good'. You see how we use the word for many different things. It follows from this that 'good' does not describe any single quality or aspect of a thing. What is good about the knife is its sharpness. What is good about the dinner is its food value and its taste. The goodness of the television programme is in its capacity to inform and entertain us. So in each of these three examples, 'good' refers to something different. The philosopher Aristotle helps us out here. He said that a good thing (whatever it might be) is something that fulfils its purpose: a knife that cuts, a meal that satisfies, a programme that entertains.

That seems plain enough. But is it? A knife that is good for cutting bread will not be good for peeling potatoes. A dinner of pancakes and honey followed by strawberries in syrup might be good enough for most of us, but it would not be good at all for someone who suffered from diabetes. You like chips and I like baked potatoes; are they equally good then? Or, if I do not like chips, does that make them not good? Or else think of that good television programme: it might be a documentary about a train journey through India. You will think that programme good if you like India and railways, but not good if you do not like them. Is 'good' then only a word for talking about likes and dislikes? If eighteen million people think a Saturday evening panel game on television is good, does that make the programme good? What if half a dozen people think it thoroughly bad? Do we go by what the majority says? If so, how do we know that they are right? Ten thousand pagans in the amphitheatre might consider the circus to be very good; but their view will not necessarily be shared by the Christians in the ring who are being thrown to the lions!

Besides, if we may call something 'good' when it does well what it is supposed to do or what it claims to do, we find ourselves in another difficulty. For what do we say if someone is able to do well something of which we disapprove? A good magician who tricks people on the stage and picks their pockets might be a lively entertainer. But what if he transfers his skills to the town centre on market day — what if it is your pocket he picks! Then you would hesitate before calling him 'good'. Is a 'good murderer' a successful murderer, a 'good liar' a successful liar?

'Good' not the name of a quality

A moment's thought shows then that 'good' is not the name of any particular quality or aspect of a thing. We see that being able to pick pockets might be considered good when it is done on the stage, for entertainment; but it is not good when it is done by a criminal in the market-place. And we all differ in our estimate of quite ordinary, non-criminal, things. As we noticed, you like chips and I like baked potatoes. One person likes Turkish Delight, another prefers Caramel Cream. Even *the same thing* can be both good and not good. Butter, for example, is good because it provides Vitamins A and D but it is not good (according to some nutritionists) because it helps clog the arteries with cholesterol. A sip of rum might be good (because warming) on a cold night but drink half the bottle and you will be ill. A *little*, as they say, of what you fancy does you *good*.

Some people might object to this denial that 'good' is the name of a quality. There are at least two ways in which this objection can be put. First, it may be claimed that although 'good' does name a quality, some people simply cannot see that it does. An art critic, for instance, might say, 'Look, I have studied art for thirty years and I know what I am talking about. That is a good picture, whether you happen to think so or not!' This is a way of saying that the quality of goodness exists and that the fault is mine if I do not recognise the fact. It sounds a bit high-handed don't you think? But mere high-handedness, mere snobbery, is no indication that the objection is unsound. We must find a *reasonable* way of refuting that art critic if we want to maintain that, whatever 'good' is, it is not the name of a quality.

Perhaps we could begin by asking him exactly *what* it is which is good about the picture? We may enquire, 'Is it the line, the perspective — or is it the colour values?' He might reply, 'Of course it's the colour values! Anyone can see that!' The fact remains that, if you still disagree with him, it is, to say the least, difficult for him to prove that what he says is good really is good. He can always go on simply insisting of course, but to insist is not the same thing as the presentation of a reasonable argument. The issue is further clouded by the arrival of another art critic — perhaps this one has thirty-one years experience! — who disagrees with the first critic. Each of them claims expertise, each claims to know what he is talking about and yet their opinions are contradictory. Each can insist that the other one is wrong, blind, misguided and so on and *it may even be that one of them is right*. The point is that if we cannot know for certain which one is right and *why* he is right, then the claim to right judgement is impossible to justify.

The second objection to the denial that 'good' names a quality can be put like this: 'I can see quite clearly that so and so is good. By "good" I do not mean anything about the other qualities of the object — line, colour, perspective, etc. — I mean only that I perceive clearly and distinctly the unique goodness of the object.' This view, which some have criticised as being on a par with occult sciences such as clairvoyance, is sometimes justified in terms of an act of intuition. This means seeing that something is good in itself and seeing this with a clarity and distinctiveness which cannot be doubted. It is seeing with the mind's eye.

Intuitionism

Is it possible then that we can recognise the quality of goodness by a clear act of intuition? Do we know intuitively what is good and what is not good? Is our understanding of what is good so clear, so obviously achieved and so direct as to be beyond doubt and criticism? I might ask, 'What is it about the knife, the dinner or the television programme that allows one to intuit so clearly its goodness?' The intuitionist will answer. 'It is nothing *about* these objects that allows the intuition; we simply see that the object is good in itself.' This seems to me to be like the art critic's point of view again, and heaven help us if we do not agree with him! But as we saw earlier, the mere insistence that one is right — however polite or however strident that insistence may be — is no proof that one is in fact right. The advantage of intuitionism is that it allows us to escape problems which arise when we try to call objects which are quite different in nature and appearance 'good'. Intuitionism says, 'You do not need to worry about what a knife, a dinner and a television programme have in common in order that you may call them "good"; what they have in common is quite simply their goodness.'

The disadvantage of intuitionism is that it does not tell us very much. It does not tell us what goodness is except that we shall recognise it when we see it. But how do we know we shall? How can we be sure? How can we distinguish true and valid intuitions from false ones? If, as an intuitionist, I say, 'There you are, there's a good dinner if ever I saw one!' it seems fair that you should be allowed to ask, 'All right, but what's good about it?' For the intuitionist there is, as we have seen, nothing that is good *about* the dinner; he simply says it *is* good and that is an end of it. So the second disadvantage of intuitionism is that it does not allow scope for disagreement. What, for instance, if another intuitionist should come along, glance at the same dinner but say, 'I intuit that that dinner is a *bad* dinner'? Who can tell whose intuition is then correct?

It is even possible that one day I might look at the pie, the chips and the peas and intuit a good dinner, but that the next day I might look at the same menu and intuit a dinner which is not good. Was I right one day and wrong the next? If so, how do I know which of my intuitions was correct? Or are intuitions allowed to change, and is it possible, therefore, that I was right on both occasions? If so, then the concept of intuition has only the same value as that of changing tastes and moods and fads. And if what is intuited as good is allowed to change so frequently, then it begins to look as if the intuitionist can affix no clear meaning to the word 'good'.

Discussion
Invent an intuition – which may be about a particular like or dislike – and state it clearly (e.g. I have a clear intuition that torture is always wrong). The rest of the class might then like to argue about whether the invented intuition is convincing or not. But make sure you invent your own example.

Emotivism – a matter of feelings

One way out of the problem of trying to say what 'good' means is to say that it doesn't mean anything, that it is meaningless. At first glance, this does seem to be a solution born out of exasperation! But in the 1930s a number of philosophers including A.J. Ayer (born 1910) and C.L. Stevenson (born 1902) claimed that when we say that something is good, we are not in fact describing anything, we are simply expressing our approval. We are saying that we find something pleasing and we are giving vent to our feelings about it. Feelings are sometimes called 'emotions', so this theory about the meaning (or lack of meaning!) of good is called 'the emotive theory'. To return to our own example, an emotivist will tell us that when he says 'This is a good dinner' he means only 'Yum! Yum!' He does not mean to say anything *about* the dinner. 'Yum! Yum!' for the emotivist says everything that 'This is a good dinner' says for everyone else.

Stevenson went on to say that words like 'good' involve what he called 'persuasive definitions'. He said that when we claim something is good we are really saying 'I approve of this; you should approve as well'. I suppose we might grant some plausibility to emotivism if it confined itself to talking about dinners and television programmes. There is, after all, a strong streak in us which says 'Live and let live — one man's meat is another man's poison.' We want to allow other people their tastes, even if we do not share those tastes. Though even here some of us might still want to say that emotivism is less than satisfactory and a good dinner needs to be more than just something which appeals to the taste. Dieticians spend much of their time trying to teach mankind that it shall not live by beef-burgers alone. And we all know that many children would eat a dinner of jelly babies and trifle every day if they were allowed. But, here again, we would want to say (for the good of the children concerned) that jelly babies and trifle do not add up to a good dinner. We should feel obliged to consider qualities like protein content, vitamins, calories and so on.

The weakness of the emotive theory is shown up even more clearly when we try to use 'good' in a moral sense — that is connected with questions of right and wrong. If, as the emotivists say, 'good' is simply the expression of approval — something like a cheer — then it follows that 'bad' is simply the expression of disapproval — something like a boo. 'Hurrah for dinners!' and 'Boo to that television programme!' are perhaps all right in their place, but what about lying, stealing, torture, murder and warfare? There is something unsatisfying in the opinion that, for instance, Amnesty International's opposition to torture in the world's jails is based on nothing more than the fact that they do not happen to fancy it. We would think it just as odd if we heard someone say 'I don't approve of nuclear holocausts, personally, but don't run away with the idea that I'm saying there is anything bad about them!'

Moreover, the emotive theory does not allow a widespread feature of human conversation and relationships: genuine moral disagreement. We believe that it is possible (and even quite common) for individuals to hold opposite opinions about what is good and what is bad, about what we *ought* to do. If, for instance, I am against abortion and you are in favour of it, then we shall try to argue our case, to give *reasons* for our different beliefs. And we shall do so because we believe that our opinions on serious questions of human conduct are not merely a variety of Hurrahs and Boos.

Language and life

We have found that it is extremely difficult to say what we mean by the word 'good'. It does not seem to describe a *quality* of a thing because we often want to say that two different things — things which do not have a quality in common — are both good. And to claim that we simply know what 'good' is by a clear act of insight or intuition cannot account for the occurrence of rival intuitions. You intuit that x is good; I intuit that x is bad. Whose intuition is the right one? We cannot tell. And emotive meaning —the theory that 'good' is only another way of cheering or clapping hands — does not do justice to the seriousness with which we treat society's questions about right and wrong. We began with what might have appeared to be trivial and light-hearted questions about good dinners and what is on the television. And we saw that, even in these small matters, the definition of 'good' is far from easy. How much more difficult it is when we turn our attention to the meaning of 'good' in its moral sense! We almost despair of finding an answer. Yet life must go on and moral issues cannot be left undecided for ever. There are questions which we cannot avoid. The person who has to make the choice between the orchestra and the swimming team *must* decide one way or the other before the day of the practice. What about the more serious personal and social issues?

The politician in Parliament, the Judge in Court cannot hold up their business until the philosopher has solved the problem of the meaning of 'good'. They are required to act at once, to deal with real issues here and now. Perhaps we might get some insight into our problem with 'good' by observing these everyday legislative and judicial practices. Perhaps practice comes first and theory follows after. Perhaps moral theories are generalisations based on everyday behaviour. Perhaps, in the last resort, the language of moral philosophy is, and can only be, a more rigorous use of the language of ordinary, everyday life.

I should like to end this first chapter with a suggestion that we think of 'good' and the other moral words like 'right', 'duty', 'ought', and so on in this way. I shall suggest a working definition of 'good' — we can try it and see how far it gets us in later chapters. Let us say that by 'good' we mean something which has the general approval of society, something for which reasons can be given and something which allows space to those who do not agree with any particular example of what is meant by 'good'. It will be best to give an example.

Consider the sentence: 'The abolition of capital punishment is a good thing.' According to my definition of 'good', we need first to find out whether this sentence has the general approval of society. In this case we measure society's approval by the principle of parliamentary democracy. We elect our MPs to make legislative decisions on our behalf. In this case, many years ago and on a free vote, Members of Parliament decided to abolish capital punishment. So, according to that principle of representative parliamentary democracy, the MPs defined the attitude and belief of society about capital punishment. That fulfils the first part of our requirement.

As to the second part, the MPs did not abolish capital punishment by the toss of a coin or by drawing lots. They gave reasons, they introduced facts, opinions, evidence and speculation. There was a debate and a final vote was taken.

The third of our requirements was satisfied as well. That minority of MPs who voted against abolition were not sacked from the House of

Commons. They were allowed to disagree, to dissent; but they were required to bow to the result of the debate, to accept that the argument had gone against them and to abide by the new law. No lynch-parties!

Of course, there are those who object to the decision about abolition. They say that if you were to ask every individual in this country what he thought about capital punishment, most would turn out to be in favour. But, in the event and in many similar events, that argument is irrelevant. Society accepts that it cannot afford the cumbersome process of holding a referendum on every matter of national concern and legislation, so it empowers the MPs to take decisions on its behalf. Abolition was such a decision and society at large abides by the result of the parliamentary vote. But space is allowed for those who dissent. If anyone wishes to campaign for the restoration of capital punishment, then he may do so openly without fear of arrest and imprisonment.

This example seems to fulfil entirely the three requirements of our working definition: general approval, rational appraisal and room for dissent. Societies like ours particularly pride themselves on that third aspect because it is a mark of their tolerance and a refusal to insist on authoritarianism and dogma. We say in effect that we *believe* we are right, but we are not *absolutely* certain. We believe very strongly that we are right, and we are prepared to give reasons for our belief. But it just might be that our reasoning is faulty so we do not compel all members of society to agree.

Having arrived at our working definition of 'good' we have by no means solved all our moral problems. In the following chapters we shall look more closely at different types of moral arguments but, in support of our working definition, it is instructive to note that no society which does not accept it has ever escaped dictatorship or destruction.

It seems that moral arguments require general agreement if they are to be more than idle exercises for over-active brains.

Things to think about and things to do
  (1) *Which of the following judgements would you say was a moral judgement?*
     a) *This soup tastes good.*
     b) *It is better to be fat than to be thin.*
     c) *Sticking pins in old ladies is wicked.*
     In a couple of sentences, say what makes the judgement a moral judgement.
  (2) *Why is it difficult to show that 'good' is the name of a quality?*
  (3) *Write down as many different uses of the word 'good' as you can think of. Put them into short sentences to make your meaning clear.*
  (4) *Is it possible for someone to be 'good' at some activity which is bad? Give an example. What other word(s) does 'good' seem most like here?*

(5) Describe briefly the type of moral philosophy known as intuitionism.

(6) What are the main advantages and disadvantages of intuitionism?

(7) If you have an intuition that something is good but I have an intuition that the same thing is bad, how do we go about telling who is right? Argue this out with a friend.

(8) What does an emotivist mean when he says that 'good' is meaningless?

(9) I like 'Top of the Pops' but you do not. It's just a matter of personal taste! Is morality also just a matter of personal taste?

(10) Arrange a debate about a moral issue such as whether the government has a right to insist on the compulsory wearing of seat-belts. Are the arguments of all sides simply matters of personal taste?

(11) What is the 'working definition' of 'good' given at the end of this chapter? Do you think it is a satisfactory way of talking about 'good'?

2   It's in the book!

Morality based on revealed truth

Is it possible that the way we ought to behave, our morality, has been
spelt out for us by God? Some people say that the Bible contains this
revelation of God's will for us, that God knows what is best for us and that
he has left us in no doubt. All we have to do is to read the Bible and we
shall receive guidance on our moral problems. How can we begin to
analyse this claim?

First, we might ask what good reason is there for believing that the
Bible is this kind of authority. Why should we accept the moral teaching
of the Bible any more than we accept the teachings of the Philosopher
Immanuel Kant — or the teaching of a wise old aunt if it comes to that?
A particular sort of answer is usually given. It is claimed that the teaching
of the Bible is superior to all other teaching because the Bible is the word
of God. Perhaps this is true, but we shall want to know what reasons there
are for believing that the Bible is in fact the word of God. After all,
anyone might say of any book that it has divine authority. In short, if the
Bible is the word of God, how can we know that it is? The answer often
given is that the Bible itself says that it is God's word. In the New
Testament Letter to Timothy (ii, 3:16) it says:

> All Scripture is given by inspiration of God, and is profitable for
> doctrine, for reproof, for correction, for instruction in righteousness.

'Instruction in righteousness' means, of course, that the Bible should be
our guide in all matters of morals. So the Bible itself claims supreme
authority for itself.

It may be that the supporters of such biblical authority are right in
what they say, but they cannot use the argument of what the Bible says
about itself in order to prove what they say. If that quotation from the
Letter to Timothy is taken at face value, then what it seems to be saying
is that we must believe the Bible because the Bible says we must. And that
is simply an example of what is sometimes called 'arguing in a circle' — a
disordered way of thinking or a logical mistake. (There is a section given to
describing various sorts of logical mistakes that occur in everyday thinking
and talking in my book *Beginning Philosophy*, Arnold, 1977.)

The mistake (or *fallacy*) involved in the circular argument can best be
recognised in the old saying 'All Cretans are liars — and it was one of their

own philosophers who said they are liars!' You see the point? If a *Cretan* philosopher says that *all* Cretans are liars, then he himself must be a liar, so how can we trust what he says? The poor misguided Cretan philosopher destroys his own argument. The same sort of thing applies to the verse from the Letter to Timothy: the mere fact that the Bible itself claims that the Bible is true is not a proof that it is true. *Any* book could possibly contain the sentence, 'Every word in this book is true.' We should not feel under any obligation to believe that on the evidence of that sentence alone. I could write in *this* book, 'All Mullen's arguments are correct.' Very well, I naturally hope that they are correct; but the point is that my claim does not by itself make them correct. So those who claim that the Bible is true, that it is the very word of God and therefore our ultimate source of moral authority, must offer evidence which is not taken from the Bible itself. I should say that some people who take the Bible to be a moral authority *have* taken the trouble to find this evidence.

There is another problem connected with the idea of Scripture as the basis for morals: *which* Scripture are we talking about? In our own country there are people who belong to many different religious traditions. They do not share the same Scriptures, the same Bible. A Christian takes his teaching from the New Testament. A Jew looks to the Old Testament. The Muslim reads the Holy Koran. The Hindu regards the Vedic Writings, the Bhagavadgita, as his guide to right behaviour. All these Holy Scriptures contain quite different sorts of moral instruction; they even speak of God (or gods) in radically different ways. The Koran stresses the essential oneness of God. The New Testament speaks of God the Father, God the Son and God the Holy Spirit — the doctrine of the Trinity. The Old Testament God is one and his name is Yahweh, the Lord. In Hinduism there are many gods — Krishna, Shiva, Kali and so on. If you were born and brought up a Hindu, you would learn the Hindu Scriptures, if a Jew you would be taught the Old Testament part of the Bible. Every religion has its Holy Scripture. The question then is one of deciding *which* of all the Scriptures is the final moral authority, for they do not all teach the same precepts.

For example, the Koran allows a man to have more than one wife, but the New Testament says he may have only one. To make matters even more uncertain, the Old and New Testaments (bound together in one Bible) seem to have quite different things to say on many other important moral issues. The Old Testament says that we should love our neighbour and hate our enemy, while, in the New Testament, Jesus says 'Love your enemies'. Even within one and the same set of Scriptures there are difficulties. For instance, in I Samuel 15:33 the prophet of Yahweh chops a vanquished enemy into pieces, but in Exodus 20:13 it says 'Thou shalt not kill'! So there are two contradictory examples in one volume of Scripture — the Old Testament.

God or gods?

The old attitude of Christians to believers in other world-religions was that they were pagans, heathens and infidels who must be converted to the true faith or else they would certainly end up in hell. The missionaries who set out from Britain in the eighteenth and nineteenth centuries went with that express aim, to bring all men to a knowledge of God as expressed in the Bible. Nowadays, the attitude of most Christians is quite different. They have faced the fact that other cultures and societies have allowed themselves to be guided by non-Christian Scriptures for hundreds of years. (In the case of the Hindu religion, it is a matter of thousands of years, for the Hindu Scriptures were written long before the New Testament.) Sometimes, traces of the old arrogance and 'superiority' remain, however, and it is said that, although it is better for a Hindu or a Muslim to obey the teachings of his Scriptures than to lapse into irreligion and immorality, it is nonetheless better if he eventually comes to see the higher morality which is taught in the New Testament.

The question we must ask then is one about how the Christian (or the devotee of any other religion if it comes to that) can *know* that the morality taught by his own Scriptures is the higher and more correct one. He can answer this in one of two ways. First, he can say that it is obvious to any independent person that this or that morality is superior: he could claim, for instance, that showing mercy is *obviously* more moral than slaying the enemy. But look at what kind of claim this is. It is an appeal not to the Scriptures themselves but to an *intuition* of obviousness. As such it is open to all the criticisms that intuitionism is open to: you might intuit that it is obviously our duty to show mercy; someone else might intuit that it is more obviously our duty to slay the enemy or the wrongdoer so that wickedness should be punished and should be seen to be punished. Who is to arbitrate between these rival intuitions of what is alleged to be obvious? But the point to notice is that as soon as someone appeals to what is obvious, or thought to be obvious, he is no longer appealing to Scripture as the source of morality but to his own view and opinion of Scripture. Therefore, the interpretation of Scripture, what can be 'obviously' said about it, becomes a greater authority than the Scripture itself. And this, of course, defeats the argument that Scripture is the highest moral authority, for the question has become 'Scripture interpreted by whom?'

The second answer, the second argument which may be advanced for the superiority of one Scripture over another, is based on the status which is given to the characters who appear *in* the Scriptures or who are said to be responsible *for* the Scriptures. So the Jew will appeal to the righteousness of Abraham and to the Law of Moses, the Muslim will give the name of Mahomet the Prophet as his reason for upholding the teaching of the Koran and the Christian will point to the New Testament where it

is written, 'Jesus said . . .' But are we in any better position with regard to
these heroes of Scripture than we were when we were simply thinking of
the Scriptures themselves as authority? Why should we prefer Abraham to
Mahomet or Jesus to Moses? Again there seem to be two answers: first,
that if we examine the teaching of, say, Jesus or Mahomet, we shall find
that it is as a matter of fact and according to the light of reason the best;
secondly, that there is something special about Jesus or about Mahomet
which obliges us to acknowledge the validity of Jesus' or Mahomet's
teaching. But the first answer gives us the same problems we have with
'obvious' for, if we evaluate the teaching of Jesus or of Mahomet in the
light of reason, then the final authority is not Jesus or Mahomet but
'reason'.

The second answer might appear to be rather more promising. It is that
the authority of the Prophet or of Jesus has been demonstrated by events
which actually happened to one or other of them. We know that a
football player is what we call 'a good football player' if he scores goals
regularly; in the same way perhaps we can tell that a Scriptural hero has
real authority if he shows that authority in his life, in who he is. Let us
take the example of Jesus and see how far this argument leads.

A Christian preacher might say that we should obey the teaching of
Jesus because he is the Son of God because he was born of the Virgin
Mary, was crucified, dead and buried and the third day he rose again from
the dead and ascended into heaven where he reigns for ever with God the
Father Almighty. If all this is true, then it looks as if we really do have a
good reason for obeying the teaching of Jesus; but our problem is whether
we do know that this is true. We cannot make a simple appeal to the Bible
which describes these events for we have seen the fallacy in the argument
that the Bible (or any other book) is true just because it claims to be true.
Is there any other evidence for these extraordinary details about the life
and identity of Jesus. (Do not forget, we are only using Jesus as an
example of the argument here; we could apply the same method to
Mahomet or Moses or indeed to any other teacher of morals.) How could
we test the claim that (say) Jesus is who his followers say he is? Well, there
is the Bible of course. Just because it is not in any sense a final proof
does not mean that we cannot take it as evidence. In fact, it would be a
very odd argument for the validity of Christian moral teaching which left
out all reference to the events in Jesus' life as described in the New
Testament.

So the gospel writers said that Jesus is God's Son and that he rose from
the dead as a sign that he has authority over all things. Can we trust this
word? You can see that we immediately embark on a long historical
argument about events real or imagined, factual or fictional, accurately
reported or exaggerated. And there is no space to go into that argument
here — for this would become a book about New Testament history and

theology instead of a book about morality. Of course, history and theology are concerned with morality and they are closely bound up together; but morality is not itself theology or history and distinctions must be made. Sufficient, perhaps, to say that, if the person and nature of Jesus Christ could be demonstrated to be what Christians claim it to be, then we would have a powerful argument for obeying his teaching. But there is no proof either inside or outside the Bible. Scholars disagree. Even Christian scholars disagree among themselves about what happened at the first Easter. Did Jesus really rise from the dead and thus demonstrate the existence of an Almighty God? Or was it a vision? Was it a hallucination? Was it all made up by the disciples, even, to make a name for themselves? If you believe that who Jesus was is vital for deciding whether to follow his teaching, then there are many excellent books which engage in study of his person, his life and work. You will find yourself on a fascinating, though perhaps endless, study. There is another way.

The evidence of tradition

We might begin by looking at what Christians have thought and taught about morality since the time of Jesus almost two thousand years ago. That is, we might try to see what we can learn from what is called 'The Christian Tradition'. This includes all the ordinary Christians who have been guided and inspired by Christ's teaching as well as all the scholars and thinkers who have had important things to say on the subject. It also includes witnesses and martyrs, people who have given their lives for the faith, saints and holy people who have, more than most other people, put Christian morality into practice. We can ask the question, 'Is anything revealed to us by this tradition?'

When we look at the selfless and self-giving lives of the saints, we might conclude that here is goodness revealed — all that love and self-sacrifice, that kindness and care for the sick and the needy. Most of us would want to say that these things are good in themselves; no one wishes to take away from the good acts of good people. But that is not our immediate question. Look back at the title of this chapter and remember that our question is whether there is any single infallible and revealed origin of moral goodness. When we look at the lives of the saints, we are apt to think that perhaps there is. But the problem we had about deciding which Scriptures to accept as the true guides to conduct arises again in the case of the saints. For we soon see that Christians have no monopoly of goodness; there are good people in all religions; there are good people who would not claim to accept any religion. No one can point to an act of virtue or kindness and say that that act shows the Christian revelation to be true. If a Muslim, for instance, commits *the same* act of virtue, are we to claim then that it shows the Muslim revelation to be true? We cannot make both claims because the Muslim and Christian accounts of virtue are different. We cannot even make one of the claims, because if identical acts of kindness can be performed in the name of any religion or none, then the final source of authority for such acts cannot belong with any *particular* religion. To take a practical example: during the First World War, the *atheist* philosopher Bertrand Russell (1872-1970) went to prison on account of his pacifism, but many *Christians* did exactly the same thing. The fact is that neither Russell's atheistic beliefs nor the other people's Christian ones were proved right by this particular action. It remains true that brave men and women are often brave *because* of their religious beliefs.

In a sense, all exercises in standing back from the whole problem of religious and moral teachings and evaluating them as if we were, all of us, entirely independent judges is a misleading picture. We are all born and brought up within a particular tradition whether we like it or not. The facts of history can no more be avoided than the fact that one is born with blue eyes or brown eyes. We might start to analyse and evaluate the customs by which we have been raised, but we cannot deny *the fact* that we have been so raised and that we have arrived at our moral opinions by means of these customs. If we now choose to accept or to reject the tradition according to which we have been brought up — Christianity, Islam, Humanism — the fact remains that we must make a conscious choice to do so. There will, in all sane and thoughtful people, be reasons for this choice. Reason is the only method of procedure open to us. Revelation seems to be a dead-end because of quarrels about which so-called 'revelation' is correct, as well as because of inconsistencies even within a particular revelation itself and the fact that the same moral act may be performed by believers in quite different religious and moral systems. Indeed, some would claim that the whole idea of revelation is a non-starter. It is quite a subtle argument and it goes like this: If I can ask whether there is such a thing as revelation, then it follows that there cannot be, for if anything were revealed then I could not sensibly doubt it (for the very meaning of 'revelation' is so clear and distinct as to prohibit the possibility of doubt); because, therefore, I can sensibly doubt that any revelation has in fact taken place, it follows that it has not taken place. If, on the other hand, I am relying on someone else's experience of revelation, then there can be no more certainty about the reality of that experience than the certainty which I may or may not have about whether that other person is mistaken or not.

This is not to say that all religions are useless as guides to conduct, only that *proof* in the matter of religion is very hard to come by. For instance, we might find — and as a matter of fact many people the world over do find — that the rules and commandments of religion with regard to morality are a most useful guide. We may discover that such practices as respect

for others, unselfishness, mercy, forgiveness and so on really do help
society to hold together in some sort of harmony. But this discovery is not
a proof that these moral practices have ever been revealed as good. As we
have seen, anyone is free to doubt whether any particular practice which is
alleged to have been revealed as good is *actually* good. Moreover, many
have arrived at similar moral principles to those supported by religion
without themselves accepting the tenets of religion. As we saw in the case
of Bertrand Russell, it is possible to be a pacifist on grounds other than
those traditionally suggested by Christianity.

If it is difficult to see what can be meant by 'revealed truth' in the face
of so many 'revealed truths' which seem at odds with one another, and if,
as has been suggested, it is difficult to understand the concept of
revelation, is there yet guidance in matters of morals which is so clear
that no reasonable man can doubt it? This leads into the subject of our
next chapter.

Things to think about and things to do
 (1) *Invent an argument which is an 'argument in a circle'.*
 (2) *What is wrong with arguments of this sort?*
 (3) *What should we conclude about the authority of Scripture if Islamic
     Scripture commands something contradictory to what is
     commanded in Christian Scripture?*
 (4) *'Love your neighbour and hate your enemy'. 'Love your enemies.'
     How are we to judge between these two statements which both
     occur in the same Bible?*
 (5) *How could we ever be certain that a particular truth has been
     revealed?*
 (6) *Read the accounts of Jesus' resurrection at the end of each of the
     four gospels. Jot down the main points made by each gospel writer.
     Is there a sense in which we might call all these accounts 'true'?*
 (7) *Are the lives of the saints and of thousands of good men and women
     evidence for the truth of Christianity's moral teaching?*
 (8) *What are the lives of thousands of good Muslims evidence of?*
 (9) *What does it mean to belong to a tradition? Has tradition a value?*
(10) *Must reason always be opposed to revelation?*

3 Natural law

When we look at the world and our own part in it, we seem to see certain regularities which may be described as natural laws. The sun rises every morning and sets every night. Winter follows summer. Trees take leaf. The tide rolls in twice a day. It rains — and so on. Famous philosophers (like Thomas Aquinas 1226-1274) have believed that the natural law is ordained by God since he made all that there is. But, whether we believe that God is the author of order in the world or not, we are bound to believe that our contravention of regularities leads often to unhappy consequences. It is not only the falling apple which hits the ground, but if you tumble out of the tree you will land with a bump. Gravity is no respecter of persons. It is a rule which scarcely allows of exceptions and which, therefore, seems to be a definite law.

It is a mistake, however, to think of natural law as if it were something like the law of the land, the rules of netball or school rules. All these types of law and rule are first invented by human beings, then put into operation and finally those who break the law are punished or else disqualified in some way. Natural laws, on the other hand, are not invented by human beings; they are simply 'the way things are'. That is why I began by encouraging us to think about them in terms of observable regularities. Of course, if we go against these regularities the result will be similar to the result we would expect if we were to go against a man-made law. Drowning at sea can look much like punishment for putting out when the tide was in the wrong direction or when the weather was stormy. And natural law seems to give us signs similar to man-made laws: 'Trespassers will be prosecuted' says the notice at the edge of the field; 'Do not put out to sea' seems to say the stormy weather. The difference is that in the first place the law is quite arbitrary — a new owner might decide to take down the notice so that ramblers may enjoy free access to his territory; but in the second place the law would seem to exist whether anyone had bothered to put it into words or not — a storm at sea is *always* a sign of danger. Certain people may be exempted from the requirements of man-made laws but natural law is binding on everyone. The owner of the land is not prohibited by the law about trespassing; but a storm at sea is a peril to everyone.

Those who accept the existence of natural laws believe that all problems about defining what 'good' means can be solved by discovering what 'natural' means. That is, if a thing is natural then it is good. There was a philosopher called William of Occam (?1290-1346) and he claimed that 'entities should not be multiplied more than is strictly necessary'. He meant that, when trying to work out any problem by natural reason, we should try to get by with as few unknown quantities as possible. Anyone who has tried to solve equations which contain two or three 'unknowns' will immediately appreciate the sense in what Occam said. This principle of cutting out unknowns has been described as Occam's Razor. The advantage of the theory of natural law is that it enables us to leave out of our discussion of morals all those questions about supernatural beings, God, revelation and the like that we came across in the last chapter. (But note, we are not forced by the theory of natural law to deny the existence of God. We may believe, as Thomas Aquinas did, that natural law is part of God's Law.) The theory of natural law is an attempt to demystify moral philosophy. It says in effect, 'Look, here is all the information you require in order to know what is good. Reason and the regularities of the natural world should be your guide.'

So goodness is to be found in following the laws of nature. It is only when man goes against what is natural that he becomes unhappy and gets himself into moral difficulties. The first natural law is that of self-preservation. It is obviously the first law because without it we would not exist to observe any of the other laws! It is alleged that nature tells us all we need to do in order to survive. We need food, exercise and sleep — a moderate amount of each. Too little food and we starve. Too much exercise and we strain ourselves. Too little sleep and we have not the energy either to exercise or to hunt for food. So 'good' becomes defined as that which prolongs man's healthy life and ensures procreation and the survival of the species. It is alleged that natural law can be discovered by all men in all ages by the light of the unaided reason. We look at the world and at ourselves; we see which activities are necessary for survival and the avoidance of pain and disease; we pursue these activities and in so doing we fulfil the natural law. If we go against our reasonable understanding of what is good for us, then we must suffer the natural consequences. If you eat too much trifle you will be sick.

Natural law and society

Supporters of natural law argue, with some justification, that most if not all societies have in fact based their morality on natural law even if they have not always done so in theory. Let us take a single example of a human activity and see how it squares up to the natural law. Consider the activity of stealing — taking what does not belong to you. Stealing is against the law in all societies because it goes against the natural right of a person to work, earn money and enjoy without hindrance the possessions which he buys with his money. Work is the natural order of things. Moreover, reason tells us that if stealing were not prohibited then society would soon become disordered. There would be no incentive to work since anything one earned was liable to be stolen. If no one worked, nothing would be produced. If nothing were produced — no food, fire or shelter — then not only human society but human life itself would be in danger. Clearly then, stealing is outlawed because it is a natural evil. It is interesting to note that in the Middle Ages interest on money lent was regarded as being against natural law.

At the Third Lateran Council in 1179 it was decreed that money is a 'barren' quality, that is a token equivalent only and exactly to what it is exchanged for. So, for example, if you borrowed a tonne of potatoes from me, then in the normal course of events you would be required only to give back a tonne — no more and no less. The invention of money was regarded as a mere convenience, it being easier to carry about a ten-pound note than a sack of potatoes. It was argued that if ten pounds was paid for a sack of potatoes then ten pounds was always the value of that sack. If I were to lend you ten pounds instead of the sack of potatoes, then you would owe me ten pounds and ten pounds only. Profiteering and interest charges on money were both disallowed as unnatural and therefore unjust.

In the same way, murder and adultery are condemned as immoral. The supporters of natural law can point with satisfaction to the fact that most societies have forbidden these practices. The ancient code of the Emperor Hammurabi, the Ten Commandments and the secular laws of all civilised nations are agreed that murder must be severely punished. And most societies recognise the immorality of adultery by giving the injured party the chance of a divorce. The natural reason affirms that a society which prohibits theft, adultery and murder is a safer and a happier society.

Is what is natural always good?

The most important advantage of the doctrine of natural law is that it takes morality out of the airy-fairy world of speculation about the supernatural causes of events and roots it in the world of everyday experience. It points to certain physical facts and says that these in themselves are good while others are certainly bad. And by 'good' it means good for mankind, promoting life and health and so on. But is what is natural always the same as what is good?

This question can be raised in connection with the general problem of abortion. Traditionally, supporters of natural law argue that abortion is always wrong because it denies a fundamental natural right, the right to life. But suppose we have a pregnancy which, if allowed to continue to birth, would result in the death of the mother. What has the doctrine of natural law to say in this case? The usual argument is that since the unborn baby is already alive, to kill it would be murder and therefore wrong, against the natural law. If we say, 'But the continuation of the pregnancy will result in the death of the mother and to know this and still allow the pregnancy to follow its course is the same thing as murdering the mother' — the supporter of natural law will reply that allowing someone to die is not the same thing as murder. If events were allowed to take their *natural* course, the mother would die *according to nature* and the baby would live. We might argue that this is preposterous. We might advance several powerful arguments:

(1) The unborn child has only a basic, rudimentary existence; the mother is a developed human being. Therefore, the mother's life is worth more than that of the baby. Therefore, if it is a matter of choice, she should live and the baby should die.

(2) The mother has established relationships with other human beings, her husband and family. The death of the mother will cause more pain, grief and hardship to the family than the death of the baby will cause to those same people.

(3) Because of the mother's weakness, the baby might die at birth in any case.

(4) If the mother dies, there will be no one to look after the baby.

But the supporter of natural law will say that all these considerations are subordinate to the overriding fact of the baby's existence and its consequent right to life. But what about the mother's right to life? The naturalist answer is simple: 'Her life is being ended naturally, according to the process of nature. To kill the baby is an unnatural act. It is therefore wrong.' We might agree that to kill the foetus is an evil act, but we might also want to say that to allow the mother to die, when her death can be prevented, is a greater evil. We should therefore choose the lesser of the two evils. For the natural law supporter this distinction simply does not arise. And it does not arise *because what happens in nature is counted as the definition of what ought to happen in morality*. The mother's death is natural and therefore right; the baby's death is unnaturally contrived and therefore wrong. That, as far as the supporter of natural law is concerned, is the end of the matter.

The argument is very difficult but perhaps it might be claimed that by 'additions' to nature man's lot is improved. Suppose a human life can be saved if and only if the extremely ill patient is transported three thousand miles in quick time to an advanced hospital in America. The only known means of such swift transportation is by flight. But is it natural for men to fly? Is not there a clear sense in which aircraft are against nature? (The old saying, 'If man had been intended to fly, nature would have given him wings.') It appears that the supporter of natural law is in a dilemma, for he believes that, all things being equal, it is always right to try to save life; and yet aeroplanes are not found in nature. But he will reply that this is no real difficulty because, according to the doctrine of natural law, man is allowed by his natural intelligence to devise ways of promoting and preserving his natural life. Aircraft are only the last in a long line of reasonable inventions which began with clothes and shelters and which culminates in our own time with anaesthetics and antibiotics. (An interesting side issue: Is the supporter of natural law obliged to forgo all antibiotics, since these destroy bacteria and bacteria may be called 'life'? The answer would be 'no', because, while they might be 'life' they are not human life and it is the business of natural law to defend human life. This is why it is permissible to kill and eat animals.)

Here are two more illustrations of how the philosophy of natural law works in moral predicaments. The first is from fiction, from Nicholas Monsarrat's famous book *The Cruel Sea*. The Captain of an Allied ship during the Second World War is sailing through enemy waters. He knows that he is within range of the enemy's submarines. Some of his own men are overboard and floundering in the water. The Captain must decide: should he stop the ship and pick up his men, thereby risking his ship and the lives of all his crew; or should he reluctantly proceed and leave the men in the water to drown? In the hope of preserving the lives of the majority of sailors — i.e. those on board ship — the Captain gives the order 'Full Ahead!' knowing that in so doing he is condemning the men in the water to certain death. His argument was simply that, if he stopped to pick up the men overboard, his whole crew would likely meet death from the enemy's torpedos. He weighed the certain deaths of the few men in the water against the very probable deaths of the many men on board ship and decided that the men in the water must be sacrificed. Even in fiction, this is a terrible decision to have to make. We may assume that in wartime it is the sort of decision which has to be taken frequently. The Captain decided as he did, not out of callousness towards the lives of the men in the sea, but between two evils. Many will say that he chose rightly. But the supporters of natural law are bound to believe that he chose wrongly, for while there was the chance of saving *all* lives (by stopping and picking up the men-overboard and risking a torpedo hit) that chance should have been taken. It was wrong, because against natural law, to leave men to certain death when there existed the chance to save them. It is interesting to note that the *actual* consequences of a decision to stop the boat and pick up the men in the sea are of no interest to the supporter of natural law. Even if the Captain had done this and his fears had been realised, all the crew being blown up with the ship, natural law would still have dictated that the ship be stopped and the risk taken. It is the decision itself that counts. Morality consists in keeping the law and the law teaches clearly that to take life in the way that the Captain did — by surely and certainly leaving the men in the water to inevitable death — is morally wrong.

The second illustration is a matter of recorded history. Soon after the end of the Second World War — in fact this time, not in a novel — the members of Oxford colleges met to confer honorary degrees upon certain people who had done distinguished work in the arts and in public service.

One of the persons nominated for a degree was the then President of the United States of America. Now these honorary degree nominations usually simply go through 'on the nod'. A secretary calls out one name after another and the voting members shout 'Aye' in agreement. The meeting was proceeding in the usual fashion until it came to the President's name. Abruptly, a lady philosopher called Elizabeth Anscombe shouted 'No!' When asked the reason for this unusual interruption, Miss Anscombe replied that the President was the one who had given the word of command for the atomic bombs to be dropped on Hiroshima and Nagasaki in 1945. In those explosions many thousands of innocent people were killed. Miss Anscombe was a supporter of the doctrine of natural law and she said that it is *always* wrong to kill innocent people; the President had killed innocent people and therefore he should not be awarded the honorary degree, a mark of the University's respect.

Other philosophical arguments were put to Miss Anscombe. For instance, it was said that the dropping of the atomic bombs forced the Japanese surrender and thus shortened the war thereby saving many lives on both sides. It was claimed that the dropping of the bombs was the lesser of two evils. Miss Anscombe would have none of this. She said that nothing could justify the killing of the innocent. It was better to suffer a long drawn out war than go against the natural law which forbids indiscriminate killing. People asked her to look again at the other side of the issue. A great many lives had been saved as a result of the bombing. Miss Anscombe was not interested in results, in consequences; for her, nothing could justify an act that was wrong in itself — the killing of innocent people.

These two examples, and the views of natural law supporters on abortion, represent this sort of moral philosophy as always adopting an extreme position. Actions seem to be black or white so far as their morality is concerned. Abortion is said to be *always* wrong. So is the killing of innocent people and so on. Charges of extremism do not bother natural law supporters; they simply claim that, of course, they are extremely right. However, certain criticisms of the philosophy of natural law are often made and we shall have a look at some of these criticisms now.

Criticisms

Natural law claims that what is natural is good. As we have seen, this doctrine has the advantage of rooting moral reasoning firmly in everyday experience, but it is open to criticisms which question the meaning of 'natural'. If 'natural' is defined as 'what is found in nature' then it seems that there is at least the possibility of asking whether everything that is found in nature is in fact good. If we can find an exception, then obviously the doctrine of natural law breaks down — i.e. not everything that is natural is good. If we can find no exception, if 'natural' always means exactly what 'good' means, then to say that what is natural is good is simply to repeat oneself. This is called tautology. No new information is given. The person who defines 'natural' entirely in terms of 'good' might just as well say that what is natural is natural and what is good is good. And that, of course, tells us nothing. It is vain repetition. Moreover, if someone simply persists in defining what is good as what is natural, what reason have we got for believing him, for accepting his definition? There seems to be no good reason why we should not say simply, 'No it isn't. I prefer to define "good" in some other way.' I might go on to couch my definition in terms of consequences or of the lesser of two evils and so on. There is more than a suspicion that the person who defines 'natural' as 'good' is browbeating us into accepting his opinion, because we can always ask of any particular natural thing whether it is in fact good. It is not, in other words, self-evidently true that all that is natural is good. Perhaps the death of innocent people, however shocking, is sometimes morally necessary?

It has been said that extreme cases provide telling criticisms of moral arguments. Let us for a moment imagine an extreme case. It is, you will agree, a very fanciful story that I tell. The fact remains that it is at least *possible* and, if it is possible, if it could happen (however unlikely it may be) then the moral naturalist is obliged to tell us what he would do. An evil organisation in, say, the year 2015, is threatening London. A hydrogen bomb capable of destroying the whole city and its ten million people has been hidden in some central part of the city. It will, according to a note from the terrorists, go off in two hours' time. There is no ransom asked for. No demands are made. The whole thing is an exercise in sheer terror. That is why the note was sent. And there can be no doubt that the organisation is able to carry out its threat for it has recently destroyed a city in South America in a similar way. By a stroke of luck the security forces capture the leader of the terrorists and his five-year-old daughter. They are held at a Government establishment somewhere in Manchester. The terrorists' leader is a brutal man, strong and determined in his own evil way. He will not give in to threats or even to torture. The Head of Security at last suggests a way to get the terrorist to reveal the whereabouts of the bomb. He proposes that the security forces torture the five-year-old girl . . .

At this point a senior Civil Servant intervenes. He says, 'No, Commander, you must not do that! Torturing the innocent is always wrong. It is against natural law.' So the issue is one person's suffering against the lives of ten million. A fanciful tale, I agree. And there is no guarantee that the terrorist will give up his secret even if the security forces do torture his daughter. But what this story shows up is that it might be right, in an extreme case, to torture even an innocent person. The point is that once the theory of natural law in morals is punctured even in an extreme case, it becomes vulnerable in all cases. For if it is *sometimes* right to go against natural law, then its *absolute authority* has been broken. Of course, even in that fanciful extremity, the supporter of natural law would insist that no torture of the innocent is carried out. But opponents might think this is to reduce the doctrine of natural law to absurdity. They might say, 'If you claim it is right for one life to be spared rather than the lives of ten million, then I just don't understand what "right" can possibly mean in your vocabulary'.

A logical criticism of natural law — ought and is

There are two sorts of inference from one state of affairs to another. The first is called 'induction'. Sherlock Holmes was forever inducing the solution to crimes. From the shape of the footprints in the sand and from the smell of peppermints, he induced that the villain was hiding in the fisherman's cottage. Induction is the method by which we make reasonable assumptions about the future. If it is a cloudy night with a driving westerly gale, we say it probably will not be a good day for the picnic tomorrow. If I work at my books for six hours a day throughout the year, I induce that I shall probably have done enough work to get me through the exam.

The key word in connection with induction is 'probably'. Holmes cannot be certain the villain is in the fisherman's cottage; it might be a false trail. Tomorrow may turn out fine; it is possible that the wind will die down overnight and that the sun will come out in the morning. It could be that, on the day of the examination, I shall find I have been reading all the wrong books. By induction we try to discover the most likely outcome, what will happen 'in all probability'. There is no such thing as an inductive certainty. This is because inductive arguments involve time and the future, and, by definition, we cannot know the future for certain simply because it has not yet arrived. We can however make inductions that have a high degree of probability about them.

The other kind of inference is called 'deduction'. It concerns logical truth, that which cannot, without contradiction be denied. For instance:

(1) 'All members of "The Downtown Cats" play the guitar.'
(2) 'Mac Drivel is a member of "The Downtown Cats".'
therefore
(3) 'Mac Drivel plays the guitar.'

(3) follows from (1) and (2). We say that (3) is 'deduced' from (1) and (2). Sometimes mistakes are made in attempts at deduction. For example, someone might say:

(1) 'All members of "The Downtown Cats" play the guitar.'
(2) 'Ron Rubbish plays the guitar.'
therefore

(3) 'Ron Rubbish is a member of "The Downtown Cats".'

Not necessarily so! He might be a member of 'The City Snivels'. In this case (3) does not follow from (1) and (2). Obviously then, every care must be taken over how we frame our propositions if we want to make a valid deduction. The supporters of natural law in morals say that the following is a valid deduction:

(1) 'This man is starving.'
therefore
(2) 'I ought to feed him.'

Well, is it valid? Only if another proposition is put between (1) and the conclusion in (2). This proposition will have to read:

'One ought to feed the starving.'

Now the issue is whether that proposition is a natural one or an ethical one. The supporter of natural law says it is, of course, a natural law that one ought to feed the starving. The opponent of natural law claims that, on the contrary, 'One ought to feed the starving' is a non-natural moral principle. There are, he claims, no 'oughts' in nature. Nature deals with facts and not with values. It is the job of moral reasoning to deal with values. And 'ought' can never be deduced from 'is'. No state of affairs, by itself, creates a moral obligation. I can always ask why I should feed *this particular* starving man. Perhaps he has been sentenced to death (by a lawfully constituted court) for torturing the innocent! Opponents of natural law in moral reasoning claim that it is always a mistake to try to *deduce* a moral conclusion from a factual premise. Moreover, they claim that it is a *logical* mistake to try to do this — i.e. it involves the naturalist philosopher in a contradiction.

The naturalistic fallacy

The philosopher G.E. Moore (1873-1958) said that naturalistic arguments in morals are mistaken in principle; they can never be right because they rest on a fundamental mistake in reasoning. He called this mistake 'the naturalistic fallacy'. Philosophers have argued about exactly what Moore meant, but most think he was referring to naturalists' attempts to define the indefinable. All simple words are not susceptible to analysis or definition. 'Good' is a simple word. Therefore it cannot be defined in terms of natural properties or in terms of anything else at all.

If Moore was right, then his words about the naturalistic fallacy make a strong criticism of all naturalistic theories, but it is worth mentioning that this line of reasoning led Moore himself into severe difficulties. If 'good' is not the name of a natural quality, then what does it mean? Moore said it is the name of a non-natural quality, a simple unanalysable

quality. But we might enquire as to how we go about identifying or
recognising this simple, non-natural quality. If it does not exist in nature,
then it is not available to any of the senses. How do we know what is
good? Moore said that we know by a direct act of intuition. We recognise
what is good in a *similar* way to recognising what is yellow: directly. (Not
in the *same* way, note, but in a *similar* way — for where 'yellow' names a
natural quality, 'good' names a non-natural quality. What they have in
common is their simplicity.)

The difficulties into which Moore was led by this point of view are, of
course, those surrounding the problem of intuitionism in Chapter I.

Is a modified form of naturalism possible?

Perhaps we might be able to claim that while nothing in nature can
command a particular moral response, it is at least a good guide. We might
admit exceptions to naturalistic morals — we might, for instance, be able
to point to cases in which abortion and euthanasia seem to be more right
than wrong — but we could never resort to the opposite view and claim
that natural considerations were *always* irrelevant. No one could seriously
claim the opposite of what the supporters of natural law claim about
abortion. No one could sensibly say that abortion is always right.

Perhaps we can say that where we observe natural qualities and events
we should, generally speaking, be directed by our natural reasoning
concerning them. This would not do for the committed naturalist of
course; he would regard the adoption of these general guidelines as not at
all what he means by 'naturalistic morals'. He would probably say we had
missed the point. But if we think we have found significant counter-
examples to the extreme form of naturalistic morality, we might yet want
to accept it in a less extreme form.

Take the old example about feeding the starving again. Most of us
would want to say that the proposition 'One ought to feed the starving' is
quite uncontroversial. 'Of course,' we say 'one ought to feed the starving!
What else ought one to do?' It would destroy not only naturalistic
theories of morals but *all* theories of morals if anyone were to invent
principles which went entirely against natural law. No one could reasonably
recommend that we *never* feed the starving, that we *always* break our
promises, that we make lying into *a principle*. So we might say that
generally speaking, all relevant facts being equal, one ought to feed the
starving. This has the advantage of helping us to work our way satisfactorily
through an ordinary day's moral issues. The disadvantage is that it does not
tell us what to do in issues which are extraordinary. And some would
argue that it is only when we come to that which is extraordinary that we
need moral theories at all. For most of the time we simply 'act naturally'.

We can think in the same way about the problem of identifying the
meaning of 'good' with certain natural qualities. If a pie is hot and

well-baked, if it is full of fresh meat and herbs, if it has a nice crust, then
surely we can call it a 'good' pie? Once again, so the argument goes, if I
cannot call such a pie a 'good' pie, it is difficult to see how I could call *any*
pie good. And that makes a nonsense of ordinary language. Of course, my
good pie will not be good for someone whose diet prohibits meat and who
is allergic to pastry but most people are not like that. Generally speaking, all
relevant facts taken into consideration, it would seem that there is no
commanding argument to cause me to stop calling that pie a 'good' pie
because of its qualities.

There is something about extreme views which is repugnant to the
ordinary person, and this remains true even when the extreme views appear
to be on the side of virtue. We suspect a system which makes much unflinch-
ing use of words like 'always' and 'never'. Natural law theories tend towards
such a use of language. We think we sense something about them which is
rather glib. A modified version of natural law will of course earn the scorn
of the thorough-going naturalist. And perhaps it will not help us much in
extreme or borderline cases — but then that is usually where we find the most
rigorous application of natural law theories to be more suspect as well.

In the next chapter we shall look at a theory of morals which defines
'good' in another way, a theory which asks us to look closely at the
consequences of our actions.

Things to think about and things to do
  (1) Are there any natural laws? Give examples of them, if you think
      there are such things.
  (2) Can you list a few events which we would call 'natural' but which we
      would not call 'good'?
  (3) 'Killing innocent people is always wrong.' Is it? Write a short story
      illustrating your answer to this question.
  (4) If you had been the captain in The Cruel Sea, what would you have
      done?
  (5) What is the main argument against deducing moral conclusions from
      factual premises — 'ought' from 'is'?
  (6) 'Extremism in moral matters should be avoided. Natural law morality
      is extreme. Therefore it should be avoided.' Should it?
  (7) Arrange a debate between a natural law supporter and an opponent
      on the topic of abortion.
  (8) A dying man can be kept alive if he is plugged in to a heart-lung
      machine. If there are two dying men and only one machine, how do
      you think the natural law supporter in charge of the machine will
      arrive at a decision about what to do?
  (9) Is letting someone die when you have the medical capacity to save his
      life equivalent to killing that person?
 (10) Are there any circumstances when it would be good to allow someone
      to die?
 (11) What is the naturalistic fallacy? Is it a fallacy?

4 Utilitarianism – the means to an end

Jeremy Bentham (1748-1832) said that what is good is pleasure or happiness. But he denied one of the main ideas of natural law supporters, the idea of natural rights. He said that the whole concept of natural rights was nonsense and that to insist on the validity of the concept in a society which could not guarantee those rights was 'nonsense on stilts'. Bentham said that we should not look for the meaning of 'good' in terms of judgements based on natural law, but in terms of 'the greatest happiness of the greatest number'. This is usually called 'The Principle of Utility' and those philosophers who hold moral doctrines based on the sovereign good of pleasure or happiness are known as utilitarians.

Bentham said that what was important for morality was the intensity of pleasure and he claimed that different sorts of activities could be morally graded in terms of how much pleasure they would give. If I want to know which of two or more courses of action I should pursue then, according to Bentham, the amount of pleasure which each would provide is the only factor by which I should be guided. The only 'law' in the utilitarian theory of morals then is 'Always act in such a way that you maximise pleasure and minimise pain.' So, if it is a choice between the maths homework and a football match on the television, then obviously I ought to go for the football match — unless, of course, the maths homework would give me more pleasure!

On many occasions we shall probably think that the issue is clear cut: I *know* what I would rather do. But is it always easy to calculate which activity would provide the most pleasure? Take that case of the maths and the football again. Perhaps I feel certain that I would get more enjoyment out of the football so I settle down in front of the television to watch the match. Let us say that it turns out to be a good game and our team wins by five goals. That provides me with a great deal of pleasure — more pleasure, I feel sure, than I would ever have got out of the quadratic equation. But the next day, when I turn up at school with the homework not done, the maths teacher wants to know the reason why. Suppose I tell him that overnight I have become converted to the moral opinions of the utilitarians and therefore I always now choose to do the thing that gives me the greatest pleasure. Well, the maths teacher might simply clip my ear or give me a detention if he is not persuaded by my sudden interest in moral philosophy. On the other hand, he might be a long-suffering chap

with a liking for argument. What might he say? Perhaps something like this:
    'I do hope that you got a great deal of pleasure out of the football on the television but I doubt that you enjoyed yourself enough to compensate for the following facts. First, you will find today's maths lesson very painful, because it is based entirely on what you should have learned by doing those equations last night. Secondly, I shall insist that you do last night's homework tonight. Thirdly, you will also need to put in extra work tonight to make up for what you will not understand about today's lesson. Fourthly, you will have to do tonight's homework tonight on top of all the rest. Fifthly, you have annoyed me sufficiently by your original disobedience for me to give you a detention next Tuesday. Do you still think you have maximised pleasure by watching that match last night?'
    Obviously, I begin to have my doubts. Moreover, that game which our team won last night put them in the final of the championship which is to be played in Eastern Europe next Tuesday. Eastern European Time is ahead of Greenwich Mean Time and that means the match will kick off while I am in detention. I start to think to myself that, if I had done the maths in the first place, all these painful and unhappy consequences would not now be taking place. Besides, if I had done the maths, I might have found it hard going at first but later on I would have felt keen intellectual pleasure and satisfaction at having mastered the method for solving quadratic equations and getting the work completed. So perhaps it turns out that I would have maximised pleasure by doing the work — especially in view of the fact that then I would not have been given that detention and I could have watched the important Championship Final on the television.
    In addition, utilitarianism does not simply state that it is my pleasure, the pleasure of the individual, which must be taken into consideration. It talks about 'the greatest happiness of the greatest number' and that obviously involves other people's pleasure as well. By annoying the maths teacher I diminished his pleasure and incidentally caused him a great deal of worry because I set such a bad example to the rest of the class. And I wasted the class's time by putting myself in a position which meant the maths teacher would have to take up part of the lesson to tell me off. I begin to wonder how I ever arrived at the opinion that watching the football instead of doing the homework would give me more pleasure! Of course, everything might have turned out differently. I might have got the maths done once the football had finished. Or the maths lesson might have been cancelled the next day because the teacher's car got stuck in the snow. All these things serve to illustrate a general difficulty with all utilitarian theories which can be expressed in the form of a question: How do I know exactly what all the consequences of any action will be? It seems that I cannot reasonably decide which particular act will provide the greatest happiness of the greatest number until I can measure all the consequences of that act and all the possible alternatives to that act. And

that I could never hope to know — or, if I could hope to know it, I would need to spend so much time weighing up the possibilities that it seems unlikely I should ever do anything at all! The utilitarian would reply that I have experience and probability on which to base my decision. I have a pretty good idea of what the possible consequences of my action or inaction over the homework might be. And in this case the utilitarian is probably right — though we have seen the sorts of complications which can occur. However, there are other cases where the issues are not so simple, cases where it is extremely difficult to predict the consequences of a complex series of actions.

Imagine the case of statesmanship and international politics. Suppose that Britain were in dire economic straits. The Government decides that for the long-term good (i.e. the pleasure or happiness) of the people, it is necessary to put the economy right. One of the things that has gone wrong is that, say, we are spending too much money abroad. So it is decided to introduce import controls so that the amount of goods coming into the country — and hence the amount of money going out of the country — is reduced. This, it is alleged, is one of the measures that will help put the economy right. And this will be for the greatest happiness of the greatest number of people because eventually the nation will return to prosperity.

But what will happen in the meantime? First, the British people will have to go without some of the things which were formerly imported, for example, comfortable, safe and fast Japanese cars which are cheap to run. That will be a source of displeasure to the people. Secondly, we must remember that we are talking about the greatest happiness of the greatest number, not just the greatest happiness of the greatest number of British people. Refusing to take Japanese cars will mean that the Japanese will not sell as many cars abroad as they used to. So their standard of living will fall and that will be a source of displeasure to them. Moreover, when the Japanese learn that Britain is to stop importing their cars, then they might decide to stop importing certain British goods. This will deprive the Japanese of certain pleasures which they had formerly enjoyed. Not only that, but it will further reduce the standard of living of the British for they will be earning less money from their exports.

The original good intentions of the British Government might be further thwarted as a consequence of the imposition of import controls. If the Japanese impose import controls on British goods in retaliation and there is a resulting drop in British earnings which is in turn reflected in a reduction in the average Briton's purchasing power, then the average Briton might decide that he has to make economies of his own. Let us say that he decides to stop drinking coffee. This will mean that the economies of certain South American countries where the coffee comes from will also suffer. A reduction in the Brazilian standard of living is certain. So the happiness of Brazilians is likewise diminished and perhaps catastrophically so, because the Brazilians depend heavily on coffee exports and if these cannot be maintained, many poor people in Brazil will die. Soon there is a trade war among the nations as they all try to defend their economies against foreign reprisals. Then everyone's happiness is reduced — including that of the British Government perhaps, because an election becomes due and they are thrown out by the people at the polls. Perhaps in the long term the British economy recovers and the people are more prosperous than ever they were before. The question can still sensibly be asked, 'Was it all worth the struggle?' For it will be a long time before the people will enjoy as much happiness as the misery they suffered during the period of import controls. And is there not more maximisation of happiness in maintaining imports and thus ensuring that no Brazilians die than there is in the application of a long-term policy to make comfortably-off Britons even more comfortable? How can we tell? Bentham thought we could measure happiness precisely in terms of intensity and duration according to a 'Pleasure-Pain Calculus'. But we may argue that this is impossible because *all* the consequences of an action can never be known.

Even supposing that all the consequences of a course of action could be known, there are still severe obstacles to the calculation of maximum happiness. One day someone offers me a free seat at the cinema and just after that I am given a ticket for a concert. Which one should I accept? To begin with it will depend on whether I think I shall like the music more or less than the film. I might have to make a guess about this and of course I might turn out to be wrong. But even if I know the music well and feel convinced that the film is just the sort of thing I would enjoy, I am still in difficulties. Let us try to measure the happiness involved in each.

The cinema will be warm and comfortable and I shall be able to drink orange juice and eat ice-cream while I am watching the exciting film, *A Hanging at Deadman's Gulch*. When I leave the cinema after three hours, I shall be able to tell all my friends about the film. The concert lasts only two hours and my ticket is for one of the 'specially reduced' seats behind the orchestra which is not the best position for balanced sound. Moreover, I shall not be able to drink and eat during the performance. But I shall be able to get a glass of beer during the interval. Besides, they are playing Mozart's G minor Symphony K.550 and that is one of my favourite pieces. Not only that, but it is also one of the pieces I am supposed to be studying for my music exam. In the second half of the programme there is to be a performance of Alban Berg's violin concerto and this is also one of my favourite pieces. It seems an almost impossible task to decide between these two events and Bentham's pleasure calculus does not seem to be much help, for how can I tell which pleasure to rate most highly, the prolonged delight of the Mozart symphony or the frequent excitement of *A Hanging at Deadman's Gulch*? Should I prefer the glass of beer to the orange juice and the ice-cream? Is it all a matter of which is the more comfortable seat?

The issue is still further complicated by the quality of the pleasures available. Although I am ready to admit that *A Hanging at Deadman's Gulch* is a terrific film, I feel that the pleasure I should obtain from great composers like Mozart and Berg is of a higher order. Bentham denied this. He said that *quantity* of pleasure was the only guide and that 'Quantity of pleasure being equal, pushpin is as good as poetry.' But is it? Nietzsche (1844-1900) did not think so. He called Bentham's doctrine 'Pig Philosophy'. John Stuart Mill (1806-73) did not think so either. He revised Bentham's form of utilitarianism and claimed that the higher, intellectual pleasures were to be preferred to the merely physical ones. Do you agree? Do you think that chess and the music of Bach, mathematics and moral philosophy are better pleasures than, say, eating ice-cream and playing shove-halfpenny? Whatever we answer to that question it is always possible that one day we might change our minds — in either direction. Then we should regret all the years we had spent in the thrall of an inferior delight.

It is interesting to note that Mill thought experience would teach us to prefer the higher pleasures. But is this necessarily true? Mill was a highly intelligent man who would probably get little enjoyment out of a fool's pleasures. But what about the enjoyment the fool would get out of his simple pleasures? This would certainly be greater than the enjoyment he would derive from struggling with higher pursuits that he would find too difficult for him. How can anyone tell whether the fool or Mill is enjoying his own pleasures more than the other? Even if we are able to dismiss the uneasy suspicion that some of those things which we dislike most are just the ones that do us the most good, there remains the fact that the acquisition of certain tastes takes time and application but provides more pleasure in the long run because it increases our capacity for pleasure. What I mean is this: you may not like the music of Alban Berg at the moment, but, if you persevere in listening to it, you may grow to love it. In which case, whenever in the future you find yourself bored and at a loose end, you can always play a record of Berg's music and cheer yourself up. That is a pleasure you could not possibly have anticipated if you had not made the effort in the first place. One part of us almost shrinks from such 'highbrow' and 'élitist' arguments but another part asks whether people ought always to be given what they think they want, what they know they will enjoy — a pertinent question when we see so much that is merely cheap rubbish on the television and the station bookstalls. Should we take the notion of self-improvement seriously? It is, after all, based on the sound utilitarian notion that our capacity for more and higher pleasures — more pleasurable pleasures — can be increased.

There is a more telling criticism of Bentham's and Mill's versions of utilitarianism and it centres on the problem of pleasures which we find shocking. What if I were to derive a tremendous amount of pleasure out of cutting up little creatures like frogs, badgers and white mice? Should I be allowed to do this because it maximises my pleasure? The philosopher Alasdair MacIntyre points out even more clearly the problems surrounding the pleasure principle here by extending the example to cover the possible delight which some people might feel when exterminating humans of another race. If the pleasure of the exterminators is held to be greater than the pain of those exterminated, are the exterminators thereby justified? Of course, we are horrified by the suggestion but, if there is *no other* relevant consideration in morality than the preponderance of pleasure over pain, it becomes impossible to deny the exterminators their fun.

It seems to be always the case that utilitarian philosophers make certain assumptions which they do not declare, for instance, the belief in a *general standard of decency* not based purely on the pleasure principle, a decency which altogether rules out such disordered pleasures as wanton killing. It is true that Mill himself envisaged utilitarian morality in a state where impartial concepts of justice held sway. Indeed, he argued that this sort of justice was part of the principle of utility, the greatest happiness of the greatest number, for any society in which rewards and punishments could be administered by the law in an entirely haphazard way without any regard for justice would never work towards happiness.

There are, as we have seen, difficulties with the doctrine of utilitarianism but, in the absence of any other acceptable doctrine, utilitarianism of some kind or another forms the basis of moral and political life in the western world. If we cannot turn with confidence to either revelation or natural law, we shall find ourselves adopting an ethical theory which sets its store by the evaluation of consequences. How can we make things better? How should we prevent things getting worse? How can we increase the sum of happiness and decrease the sum of pain? These are the questions most frequently asked. But the answers given vary so much within utilitarianism itself that one philosopher remarked, 'There are as many kinds of utilitarian theories as there are people claiming to believe in the utilitarian outlook.' We shall examine two of these variations now, and in so doing perhaps we shall notice some of the possible gradations of opinion between them.

Act utilitarianism

All forms of utilitarianism are about consequences. The utilitarian philosopher asks the question, 'What will the results be if I follow this or that course of action?' The most uncomplicated form of this sort of moral philosophy is called 'act utilitarianism' and its method can be stated as follows: 'The rightness of any act depends upon the consequences of that particular act.' The act utilitarian lives very much in the present and there is a sense in which he makes up his morality as he goes along. As the word 'act' might lead us to believe, the act utilitarian is not concerned with abstract principles such as natural law, and he sets no store by moral rules. The key to his ethical reasoning is the act itself — any act.

The act utilitarian believes that moral problems should be solved in terms of their immediate causes and circumstances. Indeed he thinks that they can be solved *only* in this way. Rules and principles are too vague and much removed from real life where individual, personal and particular decisions are always required. We have seen how the supporter of natural law goes about answering a moral problem such as abortion. The act utilitarian uses a quite different method: every case is unique. Circumstances always alter cases.

Suppose a pregnant woman should enquire of an act utilitarian whether she should terminate her pregnancy by abortion. We know that, according to the principle of natural law, the answer is always 'no'. The act utilitarian would want to know all the relevant facts surrounding the particular case. Let us suppose that these facts are:

(1) The pregnant woman has a history of illness during pregnancy. Now she is ill again.
(2) She has five children already.
(3) Her husband has forsaken her for another woman.
(4) She did not want to become pregnant.
(5) She feels she will always resent the child.
(6) She must work to provide for her family and, if she were to have the baby, work would have to be given up.

The act utilitarian might, on receiving this information, recommend that the woman has an abortion. Taking all the facts into consideration, she might decide that the consequences would be *less* rather than *more* happy if the baby were to be born: the pregnant woman ill, no father for the child, poverty and so on. I do not want to suggest that, because this decision might be taken, the act utilitarian has an attitude towards the unborn child that is merely callous. There may be much remorse and wishing that things were different, but the best result out of unhappy circumstances will be achieved if the woman has the abortion. We should notice that this decision does not commit the act utilitarian to prefer abortion in other cases. Act utilitarians are not in the business of making rules but of responding directly to particular circumstances. And they make their decisions *entirely* on the basis of the amount of happiness to be achieved by the performing of particular *acts*.

This approach is often represented as sensitive, flexible and in accordance with common sense. There is a legitimate impatience with abstract rules and principles because these often seem far removed from practical needs. Sensitivity and flexibility are the strengths of act utilitarianism. Has it any weaknesses?

First, where moral cases are decided on immediately accessible information, there is always the possibility of the wrong decision being made. The principle of natural law does away with this possibility of course by defining what ought to be done as something that comes under the authority of a rule. Though perhaps the interpretation and application of rules is not always such an easy task as the critic of natural law theories makes it out to be. But in the case of two act utilitarians disagreeing on the merits of a particular act, how is the issue to be resolved? You and I might be act utilitarians. We are called upon to advise the woman about abortion. Suppose I say that, all things considered, I think abortion will be the best policy. But you say the woman's illness is not so serious, that she is a good mother who loves all her other children so she will be certain to love the new baby as well, that the other children are looking forward to a new brother or sister, that two of these children are quite grown-up and they will help look after the infant and so on. In your opinion there will be more happiness as a result of natural birth than there would be as a result of abortion. Now, who is to say which of us is right? Remember, we have no principle for action to abide by *except* the predicted consequences of a particular act.

A second objection is based on the claim that in moral cases no one has access to *all* the facts. The pregnant woman's husband might return and plead with his wife to have the baby. The birth of the baby might turn out to be something which saves their marriage and adds to their happiness as well as to that of the other children. Because moral judgements are always made against the background of the passage of time, there are bound to be unforeseen consequences. Critics of act utilitarianism sometimes try to highlight this fact by giving the example of hindsight. Suppose the problem of abortion with which we are faced is not such a run of the mill affair as we think it is. Further, imagine the whole argument took place in 1769/70 and, in addition to the ordinary circumstances of the case, we subsequently discovered that the baby, unaborted, turned out to be the composer Beethoven. Bearing in mind the wonderful happiness and consolation which Beethoven's music has brought to millions, would we still say that the circumstances of the case dictate that abortion is the best course of action? The act utilitarian might reply to this that no one can be expected to make moral decisions on the basis of future events which are entirely unforeseeable. Who could predict a Beethoven, after all? Opponents of abortionists would claim the *possibility*, however remote. If there is some natural revulsion to the estimation of one human life higher than another — i.e. in the suggestion that Ludwig van Beethoven is worth more than Larry Bloggs — it is well to remember that it is the act utilitarian who makes such estimation possible in the first place. If *you* provide more happiness than *I* provide, it follows according to utilitarian philosophy that you are worth more. Worth is counted in terms of the capacity for producing happiness.

Thirdly, it can be pointed out to the act utilitarian that there is the eternal problem of *measuring* happiness. Suppose we had some sort of occult insight into the baby's life and career. Suppose we knew that he would be fired with tremendous enthusiasm and ambition to become a great composer but that he would also contract a dreadful disease and in his early thirties would begin to go deaf, in mid-life become stone deaf (what a handicap for a composer!) and that he would be dead before he reached fifty-seven? Surely we should not wish such a cruel fate on even our worst enemy! Yet those were the precise circumstances of Beethoven's life. Will the act utilitarian — or one of the rival act utilitarians — tell us whether the suffering which Beethoven endured is outweighed or not by the happiness that his music gives to others?

Fourthly, there is the question of moral rules. We might argue that if any system of moral reasoning is to commend itself to us, it must take some account of how we *actually* behave. The ordinary person behaves as if there are such things as moral rules. The act utilitarian does not accept the validity of any rules. This is not to say that the ordinary person is some sort of saint who enjoys privileged moral insight. As a matter of fact he himself is aware that he often breaks those same moral rules whose validity he generally accepts. For instance he sometimes breaks his promises. But he still believes that generally people *ought not* to break their promises. The act utilitarian frequently makes moral decisions which the plain man would say were plainly wrong. The only defence for the act utilitarian here is to maintain his moral opinions against all-comers. He believes that he is acting correctly; what does it matter if the common man does not agree with him? There is some logic in this position, but we perhaps begin to question an extreme morality of this type which says in effect that everyone else — the great majority of people who accept moral rules — is in the wrong. For such an extreme morality is bound to attach no value to the institutions of society since these are based on rules, regularity and order. And it is a strange moral theory that allows a man all the protection and security which arise out of our rules for social cohesion — that one should obey the law, respect the judges, drive on the right-hand side of the road etc. — and then spend his time denying the validity of those rules.

An interesting case: an act utilitarian philosopher might himself be obliged to reject act utilitarianism if he noticed that the converts to act utilitarianism were becoming so many that the good of society (the greatest happiness of the greatest number) was being threatened by the lack of respect for moral rules! What guarantee is there against lawlessness when it is claimed (as act utilitarians claim) that rules are invalid? We have seen that it is logically possible for act utilitarians to disagree among themselves about what is the right course of action in any particular case — and that in practice such disagreement is quite common. If rules are to be set aside, which of the contradictory pieces of act utilitarian advice should we follow? That of the man who shouts loudest? Or of the one with the biggest gun?

Of course, we may safely assume that in everyday life act utilitarians are neither more violent nor more dishonest than the next man, but that is beside the point. The point is that act utilitarianism demands that which it cannot guarantee: agreement on what makes for good consequences. In the absence of this agreement we are faced with chaos in all matters of morality. As we have seen, even the act utilitarian himself is not safe in such conditions.

Philosophers with a particular interest in language (linguistic philosophers) think that they have detected a further, and perhaps more subtle, flaw in the reasoning behind act utilitarianism. This concerns our different views of the consequences of an act if the act itself can be *redescribed*. For example, there is war in the jungle and we receive the following two accounts of what is taking place:

(1) The Loyal Front for the Liberation of the Homeland has dealt a powerful blow for the welfare of the people by storming the parliament building which was occupied by usurpers . . .

(2) A gang of terrorists and anarchists has caused a severe setback to the people's democracy by storming the parliamentary building which was occupied by representatives of the people . . .

The act of storming the parliament building has been redescribed according to rival political opinions. How can we decide whether it happened for good or for ill? It looks as if an act utilitarian who belonged to the Loyal Front would praise the action while another act utilitarian who was one of the representatives of the people would condemn it. On the principle of act utilitarianism alone, there is no means of arbitration between these two opinions.

Rule utilitarianism

The utilitarian alternative to act utilitarianism is an emphasis on the importance of rules for guiding moral behaviour. The rule utilitarian insists that goodness is to be measured in terms of happy consequences, but he says that we are guided in our evaluation of consequences by the existence of moral rules. The rightness of an act is not discovered by an examination of the consequences of that *act* but by deciding whether the act falls under a certain *rule*. Thus for the act utilitarian whether you kill a man or not is to be decided only on the consequences which are predicted to arise from that act alone; for the rule utilitarian whether you kill a man or not depends upon what the rule says about killing. If the objection is made that rule utilitarianism is therefore not about happiness or unhappiness but only about obeying rules, the rule utilitarian will reply that, in the first place, only those rules which do in fact promote happiness are proclaimed. So, for instance, you would know immediately not to kill anyone if there was a rule: Do not kill.

The great advantage of rule utilitarian theories is that they do away with the necessity for working out all moral judgements from the particular circumstances alone. The act utilitarian has no guidelines except the predicted consequences of an act, but the rule utilitarian can solve his moral dilemmas by trying to find out whether an act falls under the authority of a moral rule. In most societies, moral rules are clearly expressed and so the citizen who is a rule utilitarian is not required to work out his own morality from constant examinations of all the imaginable consequences of his acts.

What sort of rule do rule utilitarians follow? There are examples enough in the statute books of most nations and states:

(1) Do not steal.
(2) Do not commit murder.
(3) Respect the courts, and so on.

The extreme version of act utilitarianism forces its supporters to examine every set of circumstances afresh. If an act utilitarian stands in front of a jeweller's window, he must, if he considers theft, calculate all the possible consequences that will follow if he heaves a brick through the window and races off with half a dozen necklaces:

'Perhaps I shall be able to sell these necklaces and live in comfort for the rest of my life. I shall be able to buy things for my family that otherwise they would never have. But, what if I am caught? I shall be sent to prison and then I and my family will suffer. Even if I am not caught, the jeweller will suffer loss because I have taken his goods. And if my family discover I have been involved in theft, they will be ashamed . . . my action might encourage my children to take up stealing and they in turn might be caught. Then their families . . .'

Of course, the act utilitarian does not *in practice* go through this long-winded procedure every time he stands outside the jeweller's; but his account of morality makes it necessary that he should have considered all the results of crime at least once. Remember, he has no other basis on which to build his morality except his own evaluation of the likely consequences.

The rule utilitarian has an easier task. He merely consults the rule and it tells him plainly, 'Do not steal'. Now, moral rules or the lack of them do not in themselves create goodness. The rule utilitarian might know and accept the rule about stealing perfectly with his mind, but, as the saying goes, 'his heart inclines to wickedness'. He might still end up stealing the necklaces. There is a difference between acknowledging the existence of a rule and obeying that rule. According to tradition, criminals are well-versed in law! You might be aware of the rule but that does not automatically guarantee that you will abide by the law. Not many of us would go so far as stealing necklaces from the jeweller's window, but what about dropping litter, walking on the grass, driving at thirty-three miles an hour in a 'thirty' limit? We rightly assume that these misdemeanours are not as serious as theft, but a rule is involved in each case and the principle is therefore the same.

For the rule utilitarian, rules are of first importance. Rules were invented, he says, because it was seen that they would guarantee happy consequences if everyone were to keep them. Therefore it is an immoral act to break a rule that was set up in order to maximise happiness. The rule utilitarian regards the act utilitarian as a danger to society because, by breaking the rule himself, the act utilitarian weakens the authority of the rule. Others looking on will say, 'He's broken the rule. He's got away with it. Why shouldn't I?' To the rule utilitarian this is merely the cameraderie of the thieves' kitchen. Rules are rules; they have been invented for everyone's good. They should be kept.

An everyday example of what the rule utilitarian means when he talks about disobedience as 'weakening other people's tendency to keep the rule' can be found in the classroom. We can all remember times, perhaps when we were a bit younger, when the teacher would come in suddenly and catch one or two pupils up to some sort of mischief. One of the culprits says, 'I wasn't the only one. He was doing the same, sir!' The unspoken logic behind this excuse is that, since the rule-breaking was being done by more than one person, the crime could not be all that bad. 'They were all in it together, headmaster,' says the teacher, perhaps in an attempt to get the headmaster to deal leniently with his squad. It is just this sort of weakening of respect for the importance and authority of rules that the rule utilitarian guards against.

How strong are the rules? Exceptions or excuses?

Rule utilitarianism, like fasting, comes in various orders of strictness. One man fasting might take nothing but cold water for a week; another perhaps allows himself the comfort of an occasional slice of dry bread; another will eat one meal a day whereas in non-fasting seasons he might have eaten three or four. All claim to be fasting. It is a matter of degree. So it is with rule utilitarians. One will claim that there can be no exceptions to moral rules. Another will admit to exceptions but insist that these be few and far between. Still another will allow a considerable amount of room for deviation from the strict application of the rules.

The strong rule utilitarian has such great confidence in the capacity of a rule for creating good consequences and the greatest happiness of the greatest number that he will not tolerate any exceptions to the rule. What do we think of this position? I can tell you a true story of something that happened to me which shows the doctrine of strong rule utilitarianism in a clear light.

I was working as vicar of a small country parish. One night at about half-past nine a parishioner called in at the Vicarage. She said, 'I've just come from the hospital. My father hasn't got very much time left and he said he would like to talk to the Vicar urgently.' So I set off in the car for the hospital which was about ten miles away. I calculated that it had taken my parishioner about half an hour to drive from the hospital to the Vicarage. It would take me a further half hour to reach the hospital. The old man had not much time left. I must hurry. So I drove quickly and at times in excess of the speed limit.

The strong rule utilitarian would say that I ought not to have exceeded the speed limit. That rule was wisely enacted to prevent accidents. It did as a matter of fact prevent accidents. By breaking the rule I was weakening the tendency of other people to keep to the rule. ('He was doing the same, sir!') I might say, 'But if I hadn't driven fast, I might not have got to see the old man before he died. He wanted the comforts of religion. If I had not got to the hospital in time, it is possible that he would have died in great pain and anguish.' The strong rule utilitarian would reply, 'I agree that such a death would have been unfortunate but that is not your fault. Your duty is to keep the rule.' If I argue that the roads were quiet, that the needs of the dying man are to be weighed against the very slight chance of a road accident, the strong utilitarian will only say that those sorts of calculation are not my business, they are beside the point. What matters is that a rule of proven worth is honoured by everyone at all times. Any examples of speeding will only serve to encourage others to believe that the rule can be set aside when it suits them to do so. The isolated act of visiting the dying man (and the good that the visit did him) cannot count against the general principle that the rule should be obeyed (and the great amount of good that results from such obedience).

No excuse will be accepted by the strong rule utilitarian. He is just as inflexible as the natural law supporter though, of course, he does not appeal to any abstract principle based on natural goodness in order to justify his point of view; he points to a rule of the road that has proved its worth as a general safety measure and he says that nothing should be allowed to reduce respect for it. What is the value of my ministry to one old man if it means I weaken the general tendency to keep a beneficent rule? I may object, 'Look here, don't you think you're carrying things a bit far? I mean, I was only driving at forty-five miles an hour. That's not going to encourage others to start driving as if they've gone insane, now is it? Have a sense of proportion!' But such an objection is irrelevant as far as the strong rule utilitarian is concerned. It would not matter to his case if, in the event, no one had seen the Vicar speeding; all that counts is the possibility that someone might have seen my car (or anyone else's car) being driven faster than the law allows. Strictly speaking, even if there were no possibility of anyone seeing me, I still should not have broken the thirty mile an hour limit because, according to the strong utilitarian, I have thereby weakened my own tendency to keep the rule in the future. For the strong rule utilitarian there are no exceptions.

There is still one criticism of the rule utilitarian available to me. It is this. If I can claim that by speeding to the hospital I was acting in accordance with some other rule of equal or even greater importance, then the strong rule utilitarian is faced with a dilemma: which rule should I obey if I am unable simultaneously to obey both of them? I must be careful how I frame this second rule. 'Relieve suffering' will not do because the strong rule utilitarian can easily claim that, by keeping to the thirty mile an hour limit, I shall relieve more suffering (by preventing accidents) than I shall by talking to the old man. But how about 'Never refuse comfort to the dying'? This leaves me (and the strong rule utilitarian) with a stark choice: which rule should I keep? If I drive slowly and within the law, I might miss giving comfort to the old man before he dies. If I drive quickly, I break the other rule. The only solution for the strong rule utilitarian is to claim that there is a hierarchy of rules, that some rules are more important than others. In a sense this is obviously true, since no one thinks that 'Keep off the grass!' is as important as 'Thou shalt not kill'. But the issue is rarely as clear-cut as this. For instance, at a trivial level, the rule about not walking on the grass seems to count for about the same importance as the rule about not dropping litter. If, therefore, I am on the path in the park and I accidently drop some toffee papers on the lawn, should I step on the grass in order to pick up the litter or not? It is impossible for me to keep both rules. In short, a hierarchy of rules sounds a fine thing in theory, but it is difficult to work it out in practice. And morality is about practice. It is about the way we regulate our everyday behaviour. I can argue that, if the Vicar is seen to break the rule 'Never refuse comfort to the dying' because he is afraid to exceed the speed limit, then a great number of people might get the idea that comforting the dying is not really so important after all. So their tendency to respect that rule might be considerably weakened. Nor should we forget that all the difficulties which surround the actual *measurement* of consequences in the cases of general and act utilitarianism apply to the rule utilitarian as well.

Another criticism we might put to the strong utilitarian is that his doctrine does not take account of obvious exceptions to a rule. What is an obvious exception? It is one in which the consequences of obeying a rule are plainly far more damaging than the consequences of going against it. Although these incidents may be very rare, they do occur nonetheless and the moral philosopher is obliged to take account of them.

Let us imagine the driver of a new, advanced passenger train on the line from London to Edinburgh. He is a very experienced driver and he knows the importance of obeying the rule of the railways: 'Always follow the signals'. On many occasions in the past he was tempted not to follow the signals because it often looked as if they must be giving bad advice — like the time he received a clear 'Stop' sign when nothing appeared to be the matter. He did stop of course, and later discovered the reason for the order; there was thick fog a mile and half up the line. Yes, our experienced driver always follows the signals because he knows that his own judgement is limited by his position in the cab; but the signalmen have television cameras, radar and computers nowadays so their information is not so limited.

One day the signal indicates that the line is clear and that the train should continue. But the driver can see that the line is blocked by an avalanche a mile or so ahead. Now, should he obey the signal or his own inclination to jam on the brakes and try to avoid a train smash? The strong rule utilitarian would have to say that the rule about signals must come first. But this strikes us as being absurd. No amount of speculation about the degree to which other drivers' tendency to follow the signals seems to be weakened through disobedience can justify that experienced driver ignoring the evidence of his eyes and steering on into an avalanche! Surely there are limits beyond which rules have no relevance?

Circumstances sometimes alter cases, — weak rule utilitarianism

The weak rule utilitarian supports a position somewhere between the strong rule utilitarian and the act utilitarian. He is still very much concerned with rules and the chaotic individualism of the act utilitarian does not persuade him. But what he says is this: 'I believe that rules should be observed, of course I do. But there are exceptions. In fact the exception proves the rule — as in the story about the engine-driver for instance. When, in order to secure the greatest happiness of the greatest number, it becomes necessary to break a rule, then a new rule must be formulated which takes account of the exceptional nature of the incident.' In the case of the engine-driver's dilemma the weak rule utilitarian would probably frame a new rule as follows: 'Always follow the signal — unless you can be absolutely certain that by doing so you would cause a crash.'

We can apply this sort of modification to any other rule we care to think of. 'Keep the speed limit — except when there are humanitarian reasons for not doing so.' The rule would then probably go on to cover in sub-sections all the humanitarian reasons to which it draws attention and for which it allows exceptions, e.g. 'Extreme pregnancy, critical illness, fire, civil disorder . . .' I leave it to you to decide whether 'attending the dying' would count as a good reason for exceeding the speed limit or not. Or take the other rule about always trying to give comfort to the dying; this might be revised to include the clause 'except when by so attempting, you would be causing severe danger to the living.' 'Keep off the grass — except for purposes of mowing and cleaning.' Perhaps we should like to know whether picking up those toffee papers amounts to 'cleaning' as stated in the rule? If it does amount to cleaning, then we are safe to step legally on to the grass to pick up litter, and not otherwise.

The exceptions allowed by weak rule utilitarianism begin to remind us of legal documents (and so they might) for the administration and the development of our laws is based on the weak utilitarian principle of exceptions and modifications. Sometimes there are interesting and amusing results, as in the case of our need to define exactly what constitutes 'cleaning' in the park. The author A.P. Herbert deals with many such fascinating and humorous incidents in his book (and television series) *Misleading Cases*. One example concerns a flooded street. The question is one of right of way. This is no longer easy to ascertain because whereas cars travel on the left, boats travel on the right — but cars use roads of course, and boats use rivers. Well then, is a flooded street a road or a river?

More seriously, the laws of our society are constructed on the principle of weak utilitarianism. Perhaps 'evolved' is a better word then 'constructed' here because in actual practice, as opposed to the armchair theorising of the moral philosopher, there is a natural flow to such alterations in law as sometimes become necessary. The whole legal code is a set of weak utilitarian modifications to a very few original laws. These modifications are made in the light of experience.

Take the case of killing for example. The basic rule says 'You shall not kill', but this soon proves to be unsatisfactory. One simple doctrine with one clear punishment for all forms of killing does not seem just or reasonable. For we want to say that there is a difference between the actions of a mass-murderer who goes about sticking daggers in all and sundry and quite without provocation, and the action of a man who kills another man accidentally in response to a brutal attack. We note a difference between killing as the result of provocation and killing which is done out of sheer viciousness or in the interests of crime.

In acknowledgement of this difference societies modify the original bald statement 'You shall not kill'. Killing is almost always regarded as wrongdoing but the modified rule provides for degrees of wrongdoing. Some states have evolved a system of first and second degree murder; others use the term 'manslaughter' for certain cases of killing where there are known to be complicating circumstances. So the man killing another by accident and in self-defence is not regarded as blameworthy to the same degree as the mass-murderer.

The way in which moral rules are altered is of great importance. To begin with, everyone must be informed that the alteration has taken place and there must be opportunity for disagreement. That is one of the purposes of Parliament where representatives of the people are paid to disagree in public; it is also a function of the courts where actual test cases take place. Leaving aside the gruesome subject of murder for a minute, there was a famous test case in 1963 about pornographic literature. This not only concerned the novel by D.H. Lawrence, *Lady Chatterley's Lover*, but all other novels which might be considered relatively similar in the appropriate details. Once it had been decided that *Lady Chatterley's Lover* was not pornographic and that it should not therefore be banned, that judgement began to have obvious significance for other books as well. There was a modification in legal interpretation, in the way we understand the law, which, although it was very subtle and hedged about with lawyers' phraseology, became important for our society's attitude towards novels which are sexually explicit.

The great advantage of weak rule utilitarianism is its greater flexibility than strong rule utilitarianism. It takes more account of how we actually behave in society than of how moral philosophers might theorise about our behaviour. It enables us to adjust to changing circumstances and to admit the fact that there are exceptions to rules. Of course, the strong utilitarians (and even more the supporters of natural law) think that weak utilitarianism is entirely misplaced. Circumstances should not alter cases, they say, because this will only lead to circumstances destroying all rules in the end. For if we are allowed to change the rules in those cases where we do not happen to like the consequences of the rules, then the authority of all rules will be disastrously weakened and rule utilitarianism itself will collapse into act utilitarianism.

Let us take a very simple example, the rule about not walking on the grass. One day there is an angry meeting of the City Council. Representatives of the Parks Committee are annoyed because the best lawn on Central Park has been worn thin by trespassers who do not obey the instruction 'Keep off the grass'. Mr Seedman, the chief horticulturalist, speaks up: 'It's a disgrace! Everybody walks over my lawn. I blame the Council. Once nobody was allowed to cross that grass but then they started making exceptions — the cricketers were permitted to use the edges as part of their outfield; the musicians in the brass band were allowed to have their concerts there; the ice-cream and soft drinks van could park there on Saturdays and Sundays; and then, blow me, they let the circus folk put their caravans on it! With all those feet trespassing with the Council's blessing, you can't wonder that all the schoolkids and their mums and dads use it as if it was their own backyard!'

A strong rule utilitarian member of the City Council would shrug and shake his head sadly: 'Well, I'm afraid that's exactly what you would expect to happen Mr Seedman once the Council modified the rules to allow exceptions.'

Strong rule utilitarians oppose weak rule utilitarianism because they claim it will lead to a lack of respect for all rules and a consequent break-down of society. What do we think of their argument? There is no doubt that weak rule utilitarianism could possibly collapse into act utilitarianism and disorder but the fact is that it has not yet done so. We have all come across arguments like the one which involved the Council and the Parks Committee. We can see the force of Mr Seedman's argument. The point is that laws can always be amended in either one of two ways; Mr Seedman's Council will probably tighten up the law about walking on the grass now that the bad consequences of all those modifications have been pointed out. More seriously, a society which decides to amend the law to make it more lenient towards thieves can always amend it back again if a crime wave follows.

It has to be granted that weak rule utilitarianism provides us with an untidy system of everyday morality. But what would you have in its place — authoritarianism based on what a minority believe to be a book containing word for word revelations of one divine will? Or natural law which, in the case of abortion for instance, seems inhumane? Or else strong rule utilitarianism with what some consider to be its excessive enthusiasm for the written rule with all its inflexibilities? The other alternative is act utilitarianism and the moral chaos which that would bring about. Act utilitarianism allows for no moral concensus about what we all ought to do as a society — because it is impossible to imagine everyone in the same moral predicament and measuring the consequences of possible actions in the same way. Act utilitarianism has been called 'desert island morality' and perhaps we think it could work well only on a desert island and to suit only one inhabitant. Even the smallest societies evolve rules and it is the rule-forming activity which act utilitarianism prohibits.

Strong rule utilitarianism does not seem to provide ground for moral disagreement and for social progress. The abolition of slavery, the factories acts and the emancipation of women have all come about as the results of the practical application of weak rule utilitarianism in social policy and law-making. We may point to its defects but what would we put in its place?

Things to think about and things to do
  (1) *What is the only consideration I should take, according to Jeremy Bentham, when I am trying to make up my mind about a moral matter?*
  (2) *How can we compare and measure different sorts of pleasure?*
  (3) *Set out an argument about why you would prefer the maths homework to the football (or vice versa). Take as many factors into consideration as you can.*
  (4) *What is meant by the Principle of Utility?*
  (5) *My little brother wants me to take him out to the park, but I want to go to see a film about the life of John Stuart Mill. How should I make the right decision about what to do?*
  (6) *'Utilitarianism is a false doctrine because no one can ever know what all the consequences of an act will be.' Arrange a discussion on this statement. Write down a brief summary of the arguments.*
  (7) *Is 'pushpin as good as poetry'?*
  (8) *In what ways did Mill revise Bentham's form of utilitarianism?*
  (9) *If someone gets pleasure from doing evil, how can the utilitarian philosopher dissuade the evil-doer from behaving as he does?*

(10)   What does the act utilitarian take into consideration when making his moral judgements?

(11)   Do circumstances always alter cases?

(12)   Divide a page into two columns. In one write the advantages and in another the disadvantages of act utilitarianism.

(13)   Is there a 'fatal weakness' in the philosophy of act utilitarianism? If so, what is it?

(14)   Describe a moral or political event from two opposing viewpoints. How does the variation in the descriptions effect the measurement of the consequences of the event?

(15)   What is the main difference between act utilitarianism and rule utilitarianism?

(16)   Invent a story which shows up the strengths and weaknesses of strong rule utilitarianism.

(17)   How does weak rule utilitarianism differ from strong rule utilitarianism?

(18)   Imagine there is a conflict of rules: 'Keep off the grass' and 'Pick up litter'. How does the weak rule utilitarian decide which rule to obey?

(19)   Must weak rule utilitarianism collapse into act utilitarianism?

(20)   'Weak rule utilitarianism is an untidy system of morality!' What is meant by this statement? Is it true? Is untidiness necessary in the practical application of moral theories?

5 Being and doing – existentialist morality

All the ideas about moral philosophy that we have looked at so far come from one particular tradition in western thought. But there are other ideas and one of them is called 'existentialism', an outlook on life that has been prominent in the twentieth century particularly on the mainland of Europe. I say 'outlook on life' rather than 'philosophy' because existentialism lacks the precision which we would normally look for in philosophical reasoning, but it is nonetheless a very important and creative force.

Existentialism proclaims a radical difference between man and the world. Ordinary objects are defined by their *essence* but man is defined by his *existence*. What does this mean? It means that the definition or the meaning of objects originates in the purpose for which they are made. So the definition of a table is the same thing as its use as a solid object upon which other objects can be placed. This use or purpose of the table is its essence. The essence of the table, along with the essence of all created things, originates in the mind of the creator. The blueprint for the table, for the motor-mower and for the cricket bat start in the workshop; what they will be in themselves is entirely decided by the maker. He sits and ponders how to make an instrument for cutting the grass, then he makes that instrument. The purpose of the mower is thus determined before its actual existence. This is what existentialists mean when they say that in the world of created things, *'essence precedes existence'*. It would be odd to come across a complicated machine already existing and suddenly to think, 'I know, I'll use that thing to mow the grass!' It seems obvious to point out that the reverse is true — we ourselves construct those essences for which we have already invented a purpose. Of course, we may come across a forked twig quite by accident and decide that it will make a good catapult. But the twig was not originally designed as a catapult. The twig is given its essence as a catapult by the intentions of the person who wants to use it to shoot stones with.

Man, by contrast, is not given his essence when he is made. He is not constructed or designed for any purpose and his essence is whatever he decides it shall be. Existentialists describe man's existence in the world in a variety of elusive, metaphorical or poetic ways. One says man is 'thrown' into the world; another that man's existence is 'absurd'. We should not be led by this kind of language into thinking that there is anyone who does any actual 'throwing' for, according to Jean Paul Sartre (1905-1981), 'It is unfortunate for the existentialist that God does not exist.' And, although there are Christian variations on the basic existentialist philosophy (some of which we shall look at later), existentialism is generally atheistic in principle; man finds himself with consciousness, 'awake' in a world which has no meaning apart from that which man himself chooses to give to it. If you can imagine how Alice felt when she tumbled to the bottom of the rabbit-hole, then you will have some idea of what the existentialist means when he talks of man as thrown into an absurd world.

It is at once a source of fascination and frustration when we see how easily existentialism lends itself to fictional and imaginative representations in this way. Fascinating because stories are always more exciting than mere theories; we are more interested in a good novel than we are in the utilitarian calculus. In fact, many of the existentialist thinkers were themselves novelists. Albert Camus (1913-1961)) wrote the award-winning books *The Plague* and *The Outsider* while Sartre is famous for *Nausea* and *The Age of Reason*. But this fascinating aspect of existentialism is precisely what makes it so difficult to understand and to criticise. We have noticed that understanding is not easily achieved even when the author goes out of his way to be simple, but John Stuart Mill's *Utilitarianism* is a model of lucidity when set beside Sartre's long work *Being and Nothingness* or Martin Heidegger's *Being and Time!* You might have noticed that stories often seem to illuminate the human condition, tell us more about ourselves than logical inferences ever can, and for this reason the important contribution of existentialism and its significance for morality should not be ignored.

To get back to man, his existence and his essence. Insofar as we can derive a coherent philosophy from the many existentialist writers, it appears that man finds himself in the world radically free. There is no God. No one can determine another man's conduct unless he gains that man's permission, unless there is a voluntary submission of the will. Man *is* before he *does*. That is, his *existence* precedes his *essence*.

Because man is simply 'thrown', he cannot know what he *ought* to do. There are no rules to follow. He obviously cannot appeal to God's will as the source of his morality, since he does not believe in God. Nor can he believe that there is a natural law. And there is no reason why utilitarian actions of any kind should be performed. Existentialists never tire of repeating that man is free from all external constraints. His freedom is basic. His freedom *is* his existence.

In ordinary language we frequently refer to men and women as if they *are* the job that they *do*. So we speak of 'the clerk', 'the plumber' or 'the hairdresser'. Existentialists say that this sort of talk is misplaced because a person's being is more important than what he does. A man is his being and he is not his job. Perhaps we say that we know this anyhow and that, when we refer to people by the jobs that they do, we are only doing so out of convenience of communication; it is much easier to identify whom we mean by saying 'the candlestick maker' than by trying to refer to 'the man with a radical sense of his own freedom'. But the existentialist will reply that, in the act of referring to other people by their occupations, we have betrayed a whole way of thinking; and that way of thinking is alleged to be mistaken.

It is mistaken because, while I had no power to prevent myself from *being* in the first place, I can *become* whatever I choose to become. So I might just as well have chosen to spend my time (you will notice I do not say 'be'!) as a butcher or a baker rather than as a candlestick maker. We might pause to make a criticism here. Am I really so radically free after all? Have not the biologists told me that I am a product of my heredity and my environment and that such freedom as I have is quite limited in scope? And common sense with experience teaches that I have a greater aptitude for one sort of activity than for another. I cannot choose to be a world-famous brain surgeon or an international concert pianist! The English poet W.H. Auden (1907-73) once remarked on our exaggerated notions of our own freedom that while we tend to assume that *we* could do anything (or almost anything) we put our minds to, we are rarely surprised by what *others* do. Others always seem to act 'in character'. Auden called this insight 'the short proof of determinism' − evidence for the theory that we are not as free as we like to think we are − and, if we remember that to other people *we* ourselves are *others*, some weight is lent to Auden's half-serious remark.

The argument about free will versus determinism is very complicated and there is no room to go into it here except to say that morality seems to imply a degree of freedom. We could not use the words 'praise' and 'blame' meaningfully if we did not believe that human beings are responsible for their actions and therefore, at least to some extent, free.

On the face of it, existentialists seem to deny that man has anything in common with his fellows. We are, each of us, radically free; our existence precedes our essence; we are not designed or destined *for* anything. All this seems to suggest that each man is not only a law unto himself but that each man is an island, separated from everyone else. We shall see that existentialists seem to be rather muddled about whether this really is the case later on; but the first stark presentation of their view of man and the world emphasises our separation and loneliness. Is their case overstated? In trying to affirm that man's existence precedes his essence, do they perhaps come close to saying that man has nothing in common with his fellows? If so, it seems to be clearly untrue, for the wide success of utilitarian philosophy shows that man in general values highly those actions and rules which promote happiness and reduce pain. Man seems to be a rule-making creature. That is a common characteristic.

Anxiety and bad faith

Well then, is the existentialist glad that he is free? The answer seems to be
'yes' and 'no'. He is glad that no one else can determine his life for him,
but he finds his freedom intolerable. It produces anxiety. Existentialists
use very expressive language to describe this anxiety; they call it 'nausea'
or *'Angst'* (German) or 'ennui' (French). The existentialist must live
'without excuses' for, since he is radically free, he can blame no one but
himself for the choices which he makes. And he is faced all day long
with the awful necessity of having to choose. Because there is no God and
because there are no absolute moral standards, the existentialist thinks
that *whatever* he chooses is of no value. That is what produces his anxiety
— the awful necessity of having to choose in the knowledge that all choices
are worthless.

In order to avoid this intolerable anxiety, the existentialists say that
man resorts to bad faith. This means that he behaves as if his conduct, his
daily behaviour, who he is, his essence, is determined by external forces.
Sartre expresses this brilliantly in a little story about a waiter in a
restaurant. He moves about the place with exaggerated 'waiter-like' move-
ments, balancing the plates and dishes, being just a little *too* polite to the
diners, saying 'Yes, sir' and 'No, sir' and 'I beg your pardon' with a little
too much enthusiasm and so on. As Sartre sees him, he is acting the part
of being a waiter, acting his own essence. He has created the character
of the waiter for himself and he lives inside the character because otherwise he would be possessed with the intolerable anxiety which arises when
anyone understands that he is totally free. He tells himself that that is
what he is, a waiter; and by doing this he avoids the pain of knowing that
any minute he could decide not to be a waiter. He could say to himself
that he is not forced to get up at five in the morning, walk through the
mist and the rain to the restaurant, sweep the floor, light the fires, start
the coffee pot and so on. But what would he do after that? It is all
unknown of course, except that he would be faced with more decisions,
and after those decisions still more decisions and after . . .

So he pours his existence into the essence of a waiter. He tells himself
that he has no choice; he says that he *is* a waiter and therefore he *must*
rise at five o'clock etc. But, according to Sartre, the waiter knows that
none of this is true; no one is forcing him to do that job. He could give
it up any minute. So the waiter is living a lie in order to protect himself
from anxiety. This act of living a lie, Sartre calls 'bad faith'. We are all
like the waiter; we do not keep faith with the radical freedom of our
existence; we choose play-acting instead.

Sartre's story is like one of Aesop's fables in that it is meant to be a
picture of what man is like. It is a parable. What he means is this: we
all know that we are alone in the world without God and without
meaning but we cannot bear this knowledge. So we give our existence

to some false system and we pretend that that system answers our need
for meaning. But no system can for they are all delusions. Typical of
the systems to which man surrenders his radical freedom are the Catholic
Church and the Communist Party. They give us relief from anxiety by
informing us that our essence consists in seeking the will of God or of
engaging in revolutionary activity.

Existentialist philosophy is very persuasive because we are caught up
in the excitement and fascination of the stories and parables which form
its expression. Although existentialists always set themselves against
romanticism, existentialist heroes are very romantic figures — the violent
anti-hero of Camus *The Outsider* for instance. Existentialism is full of
such paradoxes! But there are more serious criticisms.

First, existentialists nowhere prove that there are no absolute values
or that there is no God. They merely assert this. You can assert anything,
of course, but in order to justify your assertion you will need to provide
some evidence and an argument. Existentialists seem simply to accept
the prevailing wisdom of the age and to let that stand for truth. They
assume that modern man can no longer believe in a divine purpose behind
the universe and that there is no sanction for morality of any kind. If they
want us to find their work convincing — and not just appealing — they
must show reason for their radical unbelief. This should include their
disbelief in all ethical systems as well as their atheism. A philosophical
theologian such as Bernard Lonergan (born 1920) has devoted a long book
called *Insight* to the defence of the rationality of belief in God. He might
be wrong, of course. But the point is that existentialists do not see it as
necessary to their task to refute arguments of the type advanced by
Lonergan. Instead, they imagine that their own case is carried and their
opinions justified by allusion, by suggestion, by the evocation of a certain
atmosphere and by capturing the spirit of the age — 'whiff of the *Zeitgeist*'.
Nowhere in the existentialist literature is there a serious attempt to refute
the classical arguments for the existence of God. Perhaps these arguments
are invalid and unconvincing but it is the duty of anyone who denies their
conclusions to show exactly *where* they are invalid and unconvincing. (For
an introduction to these arguments and discussion of them, see my
Thinking About Religion, Arnold, 1980.)

Secondly, the existentialist claims that the world is without value; all
moral systems are invalid. But he does not show why they are invalid.
We expect and look for an existentialist critique of Aristotle (384-322 BC),
of Immanuel Kant (1724-1804) or of Karl Marx (1818-83) — three
important moral philosophers whose work we shall look at more closely
in later chapters — but we find none. The doctrines of, say, utilitarianism
are not self-evidently false. And if it is true that man generally seeks to
avoid pain and to produce pleasure, why should a system of morality not
be built upon those two poles of human experience? In a world without
God, man is indeed the only lawgiver. But man is more than individual men;

he lives together in society. Society gives meaning to individual man by virtue of its rules, customs and traditions. It may be that all these things are mere nonsense when considered from the supernatural point of view; but they are not irrelevant to us in the here and now. Why should it be thought meaningless to live by these customs and traditions and rules — including the social behaviour agreed upon as appropriate to restaurants and the occupation of a waiter? If there is no God, then there is no absolute morality; but because morality is relative, that does not mean it is meaningless.

Thirdly, if everything is without value, then the statement 'Everything is without value' must also be without value. If that is without value then why should I believe it? This is the argument from necessary contrast. Perhaps the existentialists are not the only ones able to invent stories to express their philosophy! Here is a story which expresses the necessary contrast argument and which shows that statements of the 'Everything is . . .' type are not beyond criticism.

Once there was a gang of counterfeiters who made thousands of fake fivers. They were very good notes and no one could tell the difference between them and the real fivers which were made at the royal mint. One day an expert noticed a fault in the forgers' five pound notes and the government was able to publicise this fault so that the people should be no longer deceived. A little boy asked his father, 'Is that five pound note a real one, Dad, or is it a counterfeit?' His father replied, 'It's counterfeit, I'm afraid.' The boy said, 'How can you tell?' Because I can compare it with the real thing; look . . .' And he took a genuine fiver out of his wallet. The little boy was determined to get the better of his father: 'But what if *all* the notes were counterfeit — all the notes in the world — you wouldn't be able to tell then, would you?' And in a sense the lad was right — if all the money is counterfeit then no one could 'tell the difference' because there would be no difference to tell. But that just means that the word 'counterfeit' would have become meaningless for there would be nothing 'real' with which to contrast it. A counterfeit currency only works so long as there is a genuine currency with which we can compare it. In the same way, the existentialist's claim that 'Everything is meaningless' does not make sense. 'Meaningless' is a word that only makes sense as long as we have a standard of what is meaningful, but it is precisely such a standard that the existentialist denies. Therefore, his argument is contradictory and self-defeating. The existentialist might object. He might say, 'Everything is meaningless *except* man's radical freedom.' But we should reply, 'Freedom for what?' If the existentialist says 'Freedom to choose' then one of two alternatives necessarily follows. First, if what is chosen is not meaningless, then the existentialist argument collapses — because we have found something which is an exception to the statement 'Everything is meaningless'. Secondly, if what is chosen is always meaningless, then we could never know what that statement means — because of the necessary contrast argument.

You and me — existentialism and personal relationships

From what we have discussed so far in this chapter it would seem that if existentialism is true then morality is an illusion. But when we pursue the existentialist argument further we find that this is in fact not so — and especially not so for the existentialist. To see why this is not so, we need to remind ourselves of the absolute division which the existentialist makes between man and the world, people and objects.

Man, you remember, is absolutely free. His existence precedes his essence. He resists all attempts to be constrained or defined — except, or so it is assumed, the existentialist's attempt to define him as absolutely free! Objects, on the other hand, are their essences: a table is for putting things on, a knife is for cutting with and so on. (Other existentialists disagree with this last statement. These believe that what objects are *in themselves* is in fact unknowable. But this fine distinction need not trouble us. Our concern here is the absolute distinction which existentialists draw between the world of man and the world of objects.) Often the impression generated by existentialism is of a solitary 'I' in a senseless world. 'I' only am agent. 'I' only am free, and so on. But here is another of Sartre's stories which alters this belief.

I believe that someone else is interfering with my property. So, when I leave the room, I sneak back and peep through the keyhole. There he is, the villain, rummaging through my belongings! But as I watch, I become aware that someone has crept up behind me and is watching me as I peer through the keyhole. I am embarrassed and ashamed because I have been caught in the act of spying. But something else has occurred as well. I was to begin with aware of the prowler in my room as 'an other'; now, because I have been caught in the act, I am aware of myself as 'an other' to someone else. What this means is that if I am an agent, if I am free, then the person who is watching me is an agent, he is free as well. I cannot doubt that the man who sees me shares the same sort of consciousness and self-consciousness that I have myself. He too possesses radical freedom.

This shocking discovery of other people's subjectivity — their own thoughts and inner reality — made Sartre coin the expression 'Hell is other people'. For I suddenly notice that I am 'other' to others. I am affected by them. And they can even, frequently, predict my behaviour! That thought is hell indeed to a philosopher who sets so much store by his own absolute freedom. We go back to Auden's question which asks what becomes of my own freedom if it can be predicted by others.

One answer to this question is the denial of the other's reality. I can claim that other people are no more than objects and that only I am real in the full sense of possessing radical freedom. This defensive doctrine has an official name — it is called 'Solipsism', 'only-I-ism'. Perhaps for obvious reasons there are no practising solipsist philosophers. The doctrine seems to be, if not strictly falsifyable, self-defeating. For if I believe that I am the only one who really exists, why do I carry on with the business of daily conversation and even the writing of books, since these activities imply the existence of others with whom I am attempting to communicate? There is an argument which some philosophers take as a refutation of solipsism. It is based on the fact that the solipsist uses a language when he claims, 'I am the only one who exists.' Now, if that language means anything, it must have been learned. If it was learned, it was learned from people who speak it. If there are others who speak a language, then there are others. Therefore solipsism is false:

> Two solipsists sitting on a wall,
> One calling nothing, the other nowt at all.

But Jean Paul Sartre will not sit on that wall. He is not a solipsist. Sartre regards the discovery of other people's radical freedom as the starting point for existentialist moral teaching. For, if it is right that I should exercise my freedom, then it is right that I should respect and encourage the freedom of others. This immediately puts the existentialist back into the world of politics and the measurement of utilitarian aims and consequences. Of course, my realisation of other people's radical freedom may lead me not to encourage that freedom but to the notion that my own freedom is thereby threatened. If someone else wants the same book out of the library that I want, I had better get there before him. So there is no particular form of morality which derives from existentialism. Sartre himself rejected selfish notions which urge me to protect my freedom at the cost of the freedom of others. And some have argued that, by getting involved with politics, Sartre has abandoned the basic tenet of existentialism that all *systems* are valueless.

Being for others — the influence of existentialism on morality

We have seen that existentialism itself is not a system of morality but a way of picturing the world and man's place in it. There have been many who have tried to derive a morality from it nonetheless. There is the morality of the good party member (Sartre). There is also the morality of the outsider, the committed rebel (Camus). We have seen that it is difficult to describe the morality of solipsism. In an early book, Camus described something like the morality of nothingness and the thankless task. He used the old Myth of Sisyphus — an old Greek story about a man who was forced to roll a boulder to the top of a hill only to find that it rolled back down and he was left to begin his task all over again. This image, according to some early Greek thinkers and to Camus, accurately represents man's position in the world — that of one forced by the pressure of his own existence to perform tasks which are merely repetitions and which have no ultimate value.

But there have been more promising developments of existentialism.

The picturesque assertion of man's radical freedom has led some to a new discovery of personal responsibility. The rather lonely and dispiriting doctrine that man is isolated in the universe has been stood on its head by many Christian theologians, among them Paul Tillich (1886-1965) who emphasised the need for courage to take responsibility for our existence — 'The Courage To Be'. If we are free, then we must make the most of our freedom. If we are free then that implies that our choices have value, or else the concept of freedom itself is illusory. It is our job to discover what the right choices are.

Dietrich Bonhoeffer (1906-1945) who was put to death by the Nazis at the end of the Second World War, though not himself an existentialist but a pastor in the German Church, believed that Jesus Christ lived and taught the message of others' absolute freedom. Bonhoeffer believed that the road to freedom for all of us is to seek the good (and hence the freedom) of other people. He gave to Jesus the title 'The Man for Others'. He believed in the radical nature of decisions, the need to decide. For instance, at one time he was a pacifist but at the height of the war he joined the unsuccessful plot to kill Hitler.

The Jewish theologian, Martin Buber (1878-1965), was attracted to existentialist thought and his book *I And Thou* is based on the concept of the relation between the radical freedom of myself and others. The influential Protestant theologian and biblical scholar, Rudolf Bultmann (1884-1980), emphasised the existentialists' notion of *decision* in his extended work on *The New Testament and Mythology*.

I mention these scholars because they show something of the great influence of existentialism in other areas than that of the formal philosophical treatise. We have already seen how so much of the existentialist writers' literary output went into fictional forms like novels and plays. Existentialism may be perplexing, paradoxical and in the end even contradictory, but its appeal to modern man has been profound and its influence in all the arts far greater than that of 'pure' philosophy from the tradition which gave us the various kinds of utilitarianism and formal logic. Perhaps the reason for this wide influence is to be found in the nature and psychology of modern man himself. What kind of conditions give rise to a philosophy like that? Conditions in which man himself is uncertain, perplexed and afraid. A frenzied century punctuated by world wars and destruction on a frightening scale so that the concepts of existential anxiety and nausea fall on ready ears.

Rather than disproving the existence of God and the sovereignty of traditional ways of thinking about morality, existentialists have exploited a widespread and deeply rooted feeling that these old ideas no longer have the power to attract us. As Rudolf Bultmann was fond of saying, we find God-talk irrelevant 'in an age of electric light and the wireless'. Existentialism provides a philosophical framework for coping with our sense of loss and its emphasis on the urgency of decision seems suitable for a generation of mankind which senses it is on the edge of an abyss. The problem is, apart from existentialism's interior logical difficulties, the very diffuse and varied nature of this school of thought. If there are as many utilitarian philosophies as there are utilitarians, we might suggest with more than half-seriousness that there are at least *twice* as many existentialist philosophies as there are existentialists, because every existentialist seems to be in at least two minds about what he believes. This is certainly true of Sartre who dodged in and out of the Communist Party as if it were a revolving door!

Leaving its internal difficulties and inconsistencies on one side, existentialism is more difficult to criticise and evaluate than most other modern moral philosophy. This is because it is such a diverse phenomenon. No two existentialists ever explain themselves in the same way. Existentialism begins by despising the 'pleasure' and 'happiness' of utilitarian theories, but it is bound to adopt similar aims and objectives as the utilitarians simply because in real life human beings are not so isolated in their own self-consciousness as existentialists suggest. All of us have enough in common for us to start to sketch in the beinnings of a moral philosophy; we have after all certain basic common needs such as eating, drinking, sleeping and reproducing our kind. It is the similarities between us — similarities which are the inescapable consequences of these needs and appetites — which the existentialist ignores in favour of his romantic view of the absolutely free moral agent. He forgets that because most of us have homes, wives or husbands, children or parents, jobs, rent, mortgages and the rest, there is more to unite us than to divide us. Perhaps that is why the heroes (or anti-heroes) of so many existentialist novels are not typical people but lonely outsiders without friends, family or occupation. They wander about smoking their cigarettes and talking about their anxiety in the romanticised world of Parisian cafes and artists' studios. That such people did once exist, and perhaps even still exist, as strangers in the midst of contemporary civilization should not prevent us from seeing that the great mass of people do not live like that, and therefore they find existentialist morality strangely artificial and unreal. Yet 'unreal' and 'irrelevant' are just the sort of criticisms which existentialists hurl at traditional and utilitarian morals. But an existentialist has little use for a morality which stresses the need to keep our promises (and our appointments), to plan for the long-term as well as for the short-term, to earn a living, to provide for our families and so on. On the other hand, the commuter, the taxi-driver and the schoolteacher must spend a good deal of their lives thinking about these things. And the existentialist himself — like all outsiders — depends for his subsistence and welfare on the thousands of *insiders* who make an ordered society possible. Man shall not live by anxiety alone; he needs bread. And for bread to be baked, plans must be laid; plans which require a great deal more order and system than the random choices of the 'absolutely free'.

That, perhaps, is the most telling criticism of existentialist moral thought: for there can be no refuge in theoretical concepts of absolute freedom and radical self-centredness in a society which relies for its continuing order on a considerable degree of mutual dependence. All this having been said, it remains true that existentialism has sharpened up our sense of individual responsibility and made us think deeply about how we should use such freedom as we have. Even in this world of large institutions and corporate decision-making, much everyday morality depends on what you and I decide to do when we are faced with difficult problems which we cannot escape.

Things to think about and things to do
 (1) Explain the terms 'essence' and 'existence'.
 (2) What do existentialists mean when they say that a man's existence precedes his essence?
 (3) What is the key concept for existentialists?
 (4) Are we really as free as existentialists suppose that we are?
 (5) What do you conclude from Auden's statement about our own freedom and that of others (page 49)?
 (6) What is meant by 'bad faith'? Write a short story in which the characters behave with bad faith.
 (7) Why are we anxious, according to existentialism?
 (8) What does the story about the counterfeit fivers tell us about 'necessary contrast'?
 (9) What does Sartre say about 'an other'?
(10) Why does Sartre say, 'Hell is other people'?
(11) Can you offer a refutation of solipsism? (Try it with a friend!)
(12) What conclusions (apart from those of Sartre) have other writers drawn from an existentialist view of man?
(13) Invent a discussion between a rule utilitarian (strong type) and an existentialist on the topic 'You ought to obey the law of the land'.
(14) What advantages are there in existentialism as a way of thinking about morality?
(15) 'Existentialism is irresponsibility.' Is it?
(16) Does it follow from the proposition 'I ought to respect my own freedom' that I ought to respect the freedom of others as well?
(17) Existentialists say that I am absolutely free. But I am affected and influenced by the freedom of others. Is there a contradiction here?

6 Three philosophers

I Aristotle

Aristotle lived in Greece between 384 and 322 BC. He is generally thought
to have been one of the greatest of the philosophers. He wrote on all the
topics of philosophy and indeed many of those issues which we refer to
as 'philosophical' derive directly from him. In this chapter we shall be
looking at his view of morality and it will become clear that, even in a
short introduction to Aristotle's moral thought, it is necessary to see this
as a part of his general outlook from which it can hardly be separated.

Aristotle begins by asking questions about the nature of man, for he
believes that what a man is in himself will indicate what he ought to do.
He notices that man needs food and water like animals. In many ways
man is like an animal; he has natural instincts and desires. But what
makes man truly man according to Aristotle is his capacity for rational
thought — what Aristotle calls 'contemplation'. And by 'contemplation'
Aristotle means reasoning in a logical fashion about those things which are
not immediately connected with the experience of the senses. A man
engaged in working out a mathematical problem would be contemplating,
but another man measuring the rose-bed in his garden would not. The first
activity is purely intellectual, having to do with numbers and the
relationships between them; the second is partly intellectual and partly
practical because it is concerned with physical properties. The purpose or
end of man is rational thought, just as that of a knife is to cut and that of
a wheel is to roll.

Therefore, man's highest good results in his fulfilling his true nature
which means, for Aristotle, engaging in rational thought. This is called
intellectual virtue. From our earlier discussions of natural law and
utilitarianism, it may now seem odd that 'good' is being defined not as
that which accords with a law of nature or else which promotes the
greatest happiness of the greatest number, but which instead concerns an
activity which can obviously be pursued only for limited periods of time —
especially by a busy man. Moreover, it is a new experience for us to find
that 'good' is defined in terms of intellectual speculation rather than in
terms of actions which are directly beneficial. We might enquire of
Aristotle as to what is really good about sitting down and thinking. It
may be a pleasant enough activity in itself — a rather more rarefied

experience than playing chess perhaps — but what *good* does it do anyone
else? What good does it do me, even?

Aristotle can answer this question without difficulty. He refers us to his
careful analysis and grading of everything there is in the world. Trees and
plants follow their own purpose; they grow and bear fruit. Animals follow
their purpose which is to behave as animals behave and to reproduce their
kind. Human beings follow their purpose which to Aristotle is their
obvious purpose: to think, to exercise their intelligence, to be reasonable.
This capacity is what makes us higher than the animals; it is what separates
us from them. Therefore it is our highest purpose.

This conclusion emphasises the link in Aristotle's philosophy between
his morality and his general world view. Everything is arranged in a strict
hierarchy of being — sometimes philosophers call this order of being an
'ontology' from the Greek word for 'being'. There is the world of objects,
then that of plants, animals and man. Finally there is God, whom Aristotle
calls the Unmoved Mover. We should not confuse Aristotle's God with the
God of the Bible or indeed with any general picture of God as he is
worshipped by any of the world religions. For Aristotle, God is that to
which everything tends. He is *thought* eternally thinking itself. God must
think only about himself because he, as that which is most perfect, will
think only about that which is most perfect. We can now see perhaps why
abstract intellectual thought is regarded as the true occupation of man; it
is that which draws him closest to God, to what is most perfect. But we
would be making a huge mistake if we were to imagine Aristotle's God
involving himself in the world like the God of Moses or the Father of Our
Lord Jesus Christ or the Hindus' Lord Krishna. The Unmoved Mover is an
intellectual abstraction — pure thought eternally thinking itself.

As much as Aristotle exalts the intellectual life as the noblest and the
best, he cannot avoid the fact that man must live in the world of objects
and practical things. Even the pure philosopher must eat and drink. So,
besides the intellectual virtues, there are moral virtues as well. Aristotle
includes the following in his list of moral virtues: courage, temperance,
liberality, gentleness, modesty and greatness of soul. These are contrasted
with the activity of speculative thought and are what might be called
practical wisdom. As might be expected from such an hierarchical and
ordered thinker as Aristotle, he claims that the moral virtues are nonetheless under the general control of the superior intellect. They are not
themselves examples of pure thought of course, but they are the result of
thought's influence upon action. How does this come about?

According to Aristotle, practical wisdom and the experience of moral
virtue arises out of intelligence's discovery of *the mean* between *extremes*.
So courage is the moral virtue which is the mean between the extremes
of rashness and cowardice. Temperance is the mean between excess and
abstinence. Liberality is the mean between stinginess and wastefulness.
There is something immediately appealing about this aspect of Aristotle's

moral philosophy. It strikes us as reasonable, practical and above all
moderate — an agreeable change from the extremism which we thought we
saw in act utilitarianism and the inflexible assertions of natural law. We
should always aim at the mean between extremes, says Aristotle, if we
seek to practise virtue. And our reason dictates that this is what we ought
to practise for it is the practice of virtue which leads to our happiness.

The questions arise of, first, how am I supposed to recognise a moral
virtue when I see one and, secondly, how do I ensure that I do in fact
become truly virtuous? In answer to the first question, Aristotle simply
directs us to the doctrine of the mean: Always aim for the mean between
two extremes. But we might reply that *always* aiming for the mean is itself
one of the extremes to be avoided:

First extreme	never aim for the mean
Second extreme	always aim for the mean
Mean	sometimes aim for the mean

More seriously, we can object that some actions are always to be
avoided and that in these cases the doctrine of the mean is irrelevant. It
may be that sensible eating is the mean between gluttony and starvation,
because it may sometimes be right to appear gluttonous — for instance
if someone puts food before me when I have not eaten for a week. And it
is perhaps sometimes right to starve — if I have overeaten and so become
fat. But we object, with justification, that it could never be right to be
envious or to behave shamefully and that it is merely absurd to say that
shameful behaviour is the mean between saintliness and vice! Shameful
behaviour *is* vice. And it is silly to talk about 'too much' goodness and 'too
little' vice, but, so it may be argued, that is exactly the sort of absurdity
we are committed to when we seek always to follow the doctrine of the
mean.

Aristotle answers this objection by claiming that what is evil is
obviously evil; its name tells us so. Malice, murder and theft are examples
of possible actions which are obviously bad and therefore of cases where
to seek the mean is simply inappropriate. Common sense inclines us to
rally to Aristotle's support here. Of course, we should not expect his
useful doctrine of the mean to extend to cases of obvious evil! But a
moment's thought reveals that it is precisely the job of the moral
philosopher (Aristotle's job) to point out those things which are bad and
to tell us why they are bad. To appeal to what is *obvious* is to find
ourselves back among all those difficulties we met in connection with
intuitionism in chapter one. Besides, if there is a list of actions — or of
the names of actions — which are obviously evil, then how can we ever
be certain whether a particular action belongs to this list? Even allowing
that theft, adultery and murder are clear cases, we find we are not so sure
when it comes to telling untruths. Varieties of utilitarians could put up
good arguments to show that it might be right to tell a lie sometimes —

to the agent of a hostile foreign power, for instance.

To our second question, the one concerned with the practical task of becoming virtuous, Aristotle says simply that a man becomes virtuous by the performance of virtuous acts. Unless we know what these virtuous acts are, Aristotle's recommendation is a kind of circular argument of the type 'do good by doing good', 'eat by eating' and so on. But if we once accept Aristotle's own list of virtues as valid, then this does not seem to be at all bad advice. It is interesting and worth noting that Aristotle thinks we become virtuous in ourselves, 'in our souls', by the practice of virtue. So a virtuous man is not virtuous only when he is behaving virtuously; he is virtuous even when he is asleep — if he has cultivated the habit of virtue. This squares with Aristotle's original statement that while intellectual virtues are developed by training and instruction, the moral virtues are a result of trying to do what is good in our everyday life. Once again, our hearts warm to Aristotle's common sense in moral philosophy as we see the close connection between his doctrine and our general experience. Besides, this view of the virtuous man also accords with our ordinary talk. We feel entitled to refer to a man as 'a good man' even though he may not be doing anything which is good at the moment — he is asleep, perhaps. We mean that when he wakes up, given the chance and the right circumstances, he will act virtuously. We expect him to do so. The grounds for that expectation — regular habits of virtue — are what entitle us to call him a virtuous man.

'One swallow does not make a summer', says Aristotle. He means that there must be a continuous attempt to practise virtue before a man may be regarded as virtuous. Moreover, the question of circumstances looms large in Aristotle's thinking. Actions are virtuous according to a man's intention to act virtuously, but he must also have regard to the circumstances surrounding his intention, the facts against which the proposed action is set. This attention to circumstances Aristotle calls 'prudence' and it is a quality of the greatest importance for his whole thinking on the subject of morality. A man must not only desire to do good; he must know when and how to do it. And the 'when' and the 'how' are as important to Aristotle as the original intention. This fact brings out the closeness which exists in Greek thought between moral qualities and practical knowledge. Virtue for Aristotle is a sort of virtuosity in fact, an art or a skill where prudence and practicality play a large part. A man must, in order to act with genuine virtue, be able to judge whether his proposed action is bravery (which is virtuous) or merely rashness (which is foolishness). So we can see another sense in which Aristotle insists that we only become virtuous by constant practice.

In English law, ignorance of the law is no defence in cases of wrong-doing. If I am caught stealing, it is no use my saying that I did not know that stealing was wrong. The policeman will arrest me just the same and the jury will convict despite my protestations. The same is true of

Aristotle's thought on the subject of excuses. He claims that it is no excuse to argue that you did not behave virtuously because you were not sure what was meant by being virtuous. However, he allows that ignorance not of virtue itself but of certain *facts* might constitute an excuse. For instance, to return to the policeman for a minute, if he catches me picking up a watch from the side of the shower in the changing room and I say that I did not think there was anything wrong about stealing watches, then he will rightly arrest me. Aristotle claims that ignorance of what is virtuous and of what is immoral is itself an example of immorality. But if the policeman sees me pick up the watch and I say, 'I'm so sorry, I thought it was my own watch. As a matter of fact I have one exactly like it', then, if he believes my statement, he might let me go. I was not intending to steal the watch, and therefore I am not guilty of stealing it.

This seems just in extreme cases but what about the question of exceeding the speed limit? Suppose I am driving at thirty-seven miles an hour in a thirty mile an hour limit. The police patrol waves me into the roadside. Now, if I say I had never heard of a law about the thirty mile an hour limit, then clearly that will be no defence. Part of my moral duty is to know what the law is. But what if I claim that my speedometer is faulty and I could not believe I was exceeding the limit because I have only just discovered it to be faulty — now, when the policeman drew attention to my real speed? This is not ignorance of a moral law, but only ignorance of a particular fact. But should I not have taken account of the possibility that the speedometer was faulty? Perhaps, also, I ought to have been able to judge that I was in fact travelling in excess of the speed limit? Surely Aristotle's other doctrine of prudence would tell against him here? The issue is not easily settled, but we may be thankful that Aristotle's doctrine of excuses exists and that a doctor who accidentally poisons a patient by the administration of the wrong drug is not charged with murder. That he will very likely be charged with manslaughter may be held to justify the relevance of Aristotle's doctrine of prudence. The doctor did not intend to kill, but he should have taken more care in his dispensary.

Aristotle's doctrine of the perfection of the Unmoved Mover and the excellence of pure thought lead him, as we have seen, to conclude that the greatest good is also the greatest happiness and that this is to be found in the practice of speculative philosophy which is an end in itself — the only thing that *is* an end in itself. However, certain other goods must be achieved before a man progresses to the final good and happiness of philosophy and these goods are *means* to that end. We think for instance of health. If a man is in constant pain, then he cannot think straight. If he cannot think straight, then he cannot be enjoying the happiness which comes through the exercise of pure thought. So health is a good as a means to the greatest good. If the pain can be eased by medicine, then the practice of medicine is good — also as a means. Aristotle says that, in order to achieve the highest good, a man must also enjoy an amount of liberty and wealth.

It is in the consideration of how these lesser goods are to be provided that the moral philosophy of Aristotle has encountered the severest criticisms. While it may rightly be argued that pure thought is, by itself, an activity without limit, it does not appear that liberty and wealth are similarly unrestricted. There is a finite amount of money, food, goods and so on in the world and it is not immediately apparent that there is enough of these necessities for everyone to take sufficient to ensure that they progress to the greatest good — the activity of speculative philosophy. It follows that, if some are to progress to the privilege of pure thought, there will be an imbalance in consumption of finite resources. So the supreme good is a possibility only for a minority of people. Critics of Aristotle have argued that this being the case, speculative philosophy cannot be the supreme good. They say that the greatest good consists in making sure that everyone has enough for the necessities of life and that pure philosophy must come second (or even lower down) on the list of those things which are good. Certainly there is an obscenity in the picture of the great-souled, liberal, agreeable man engrossed in his speculative reasoning and abstract thinking while thousands starve. However good philosophy may be, it is not good for those who are starving! It is a necessary condition for speculative thinking to take place (for any length of time) for the thinker not to be starving. How does Aristotle justify the inequality implicit in his moral philosophy?

The short answer is that he does not justify it at all. Aristotle's world is the polis, the Greek city state of the fourth century BC with all its inequalities of rank and privilege, with its noblemen and its slaves. He does not write against the background of Bentham and Mill and the sort of utilitarian distribution of resources regarded as desirable in a modern technological society. Alasdair MacIntyre criticises Aristotle's moral philosophy as follows: 'Thus the whole of human life reaches its highest point in the activity of a speculative philosopher with a reasonable income. The banality of the conclusion could not be more apparent.' Has Aristotle any defence which could yet retrieve his moral philosophy as a guide to life in the twentieth century rather than as small-town ethics in an ancient city state?

Present-day supporters of Aristotle generally make two points by way of reply. First, they say that it is not everyone — indeed it is only a small proportion of people — who will either desire or be capable of pure speculative philosophy. Indeed, if the many (*hoi polloi*) were given the choice of activities, very few of them would in fact opt for philosophy. Philosophy is an exalted art and it is also very difficult (with that we all agree!) and so it does not have a very wide appeal. Let those who are capable therefore pursue it. Critics of Aristotle are not at all satisfied by this reply. They claim that a sovereign good which can only exist for a very few is no sort of sovereign good and that to claim that it is makes us view those who are not attracted by it as if they were sub-standard human beings. It divides people into the Philosophers and the Rest.

Aristotle will simply reply that, while we may lament the fact that only a few people are interested in philosophy, we cannot avoid or deny that fact. That is how things are. Most men are attracted more by the pleasures which Jeremy Bentham lists — 'pushpin as good as poetry' — than by the rigorous delights of abstract thought. But those who are capable of enjoying the highest good should not be deprived of that enjoyment just because it is not shared by everyone else.

Critics answer that this entirely rules out all possibility of education. There was a time when none of us knew any philosophy. There was even a time when Aristotle knew no philosophy! Only let us introduce men to abstract thought; let us do this carefully so that they are not put off. Then we shall see that it is within the capacity of more people than at first we imagined. On a personal note, I might just mention that my lively philosophy evening class in York and the sales in schools of two earlier books which I have written on philosophical matters says at least *something* in support of these critics! After all, Aristotle lived in a very static society where everyone knew his proper place and station and there was not much movement up or down the social ladder, but our own society is much more open. We should not forget that Aristotle's moral philosophy took for granted the existence of slaves.

Secondly, Aristotle's supporters say that, whatever the social conditions that prevail, abstract thought is still the highest and noblest of man's activities and therefore it is the greatest good. And it would be absurd to say 'This is the greatest good but nobody should seek it.' It will be objected by Aristotle's critics that he has not proved the worth of the sort of contemplation which he recommends. What if all that talk about the Unmoved Mover is based on a delusion? Aristotle cannot prove the existence of his God towards whom he claims we all tend. It may be better after all to apply our logical skills to scientific and practical problems such as the provision of food and the abolition of wars.

As you can see even from this brief introduction, the moral philosophy of Aristotle is highly controversial. But you might think that, morality being what it is, *all* systems of moral philosophy are controversial. Certainly, nothing you read in this or any other book on morals that I can call to mind will encourage you to think otherwise. Critics of Aristotle point to his élitism, his intellectual snobbishness and his priggishness, his obsession with abstract thinking and the difficulties involved in the definition of the mean. Supporters indicate the commonsensical aspects of much of what he says about moral virtue and his straightforward guidance for those who seek to live a moral life, to become virtuous and happy in a way that is better than 'pushpin'.

What do you think?

Things to think about and things to do

The magnanimous man, since he deserves most, must be good in the
highest degree; for the better man always deserves more, and the best
man most . . . It is chiefly with honours and dishonours then that the
magnanimous man is concerned, and at honours that are great and
conferred by good men he will be moderately pleased, thinking that he
is coming by his own or even less than his own; for there can be no
honour that is worthy of perfect virtue, yet he will at any rate accept it
since they have nothing greater to bestow on him; but honour from
casual people and on trifling grounds he will utterly despise . . . He is
free of speech because he is contemptuous; he is given to telling the
truth except when he speaks in irony to the vulgar . . . A slow step is
thought proper to the magnanimous man, a deep voice and a level
utterance. (from the *Nicomachean Ethics*)

(1) *Examine the passage above. Was Aristotle a prig?*
(2) *What does Aristotle mean by 'contemplation'?*
(3) *What is man's highest good according to Aristotle?*
(4) *Who or what is the Unmoved Mover?*
(5) *What two classes does Aristotle invent and to which the virtues
belong?*
(6) *What are intellectual virtues?*
(7) *List some of the moral virtues.*
(8) *Give examples of Aristotle's doctrine of the Mean.*
(9) *'The mean between contemplation and unconsciousness is frivolous
thought.' If so, is this a refutation of Aristotle's doctrine of the Mean?*
(10) *Are some actions always to be avoided? Does the fact that we
sometimes think we can identify evil actions contradict Aristotle's
views of the Mean?*
(11) *Is Aristotle's recommendation that we should 'become good by
doing good acts' a dead end — unless we first know what good acts
are?*
(12) *'One swallow does not make a summer', says Aristotle. What does he
mean to suggest by this about 'the good man'?*
(13) *Give examples of mistakes in everyday life which Aristotle thinks
are excusable and other examples which are not.*
(14) *Is ignorance of the law any defence?*
(15) *Am I responsible for what I do when I am drunk or only for getting
drunk in the first place?*
(16) *Is Aristotle a snob?*
(17) *'The ideal man as presented in Aristotle's thought is the speculative
philosopher. This ideal man requires the humble services of others
if he is to have the time to speculate. The existence of slaves or*

*servants who have no chance to fulfil themselves is an injustice.
Therefore Aristotle's moral philosophy is built on injustice.' Is it?*
(18)   What would Aristotle have said about 'pushpin'?

II Immanuel Kant

Immanuel Kant (1724-1804) is regarded as one of the most important of
modern philosophers. He did not publish his most influential works until
he was almost sixty, when he said he had been 'aroused from dogmatic
slumbers' by the sceptical philosopher David Hume. Kant lived in
Königsberg and he was a quiet man of such regular habits that the
townspeople said they could set their watches by the timing of his morning
walk to the coffee shop. In 1785 Kant produced his *Groundwork of the
Metaphysics of Morals.*

He began by asking, as many others have asked, what is the meaning
of 'good'. He rejected completely all definitions which explain what is
good in terms of consequences. So we see that he stands apart from both
the modern utilitarians and Aristotle. Kant said that the only good is a
good will which 'shines forth like a precious jewel'. And the function of
the good will is to do its duty. Why should anyone seek to do his duty
then unless it be in order to promote good consequences? Kant's answer
is simple and uncompromising: the only reason for doing one's duty is
that it *is* one's duty. The problem then arises of how anyone can find out
what constitutes his duty. For the utilitarian the answer is simple — in
principle at least, if not in practice. His duty is to promote the greatest
happiness of the greatest number. Exactly how he is to do this may be
(as we have seen) the subject of lengthy debate; but the utilitarian has a
principle — the principle of utility — on which to base his moral reasoning.
If Kant will not consider consequences as a reason for action, what reason
will he suggest instead?

Kant's answer to this question is famous and it has become a catch-
phrase in other areas of life than that of moral philosophy. It is the
Categorical Imperative. We shall try to find out what Kant means by this
striking phrase. Kant describes the Categorical Imperative as an injunction
to 'Act only on that maxim through which you can at the same time will
that it should become a universal law.' This means in effect that we should
only do those things which it would be reasonable for every reasonable
and law-abiding person to do. The word 'reasonable' appears twice in that
last sentence as a stress on the fact that for Kant reason is the key to
everything. You will notice that he does not say we should act according
to a maxim which, if everybody were to act in the same way, would
guarantee good *consequences.* We cannot emphasise too much Kant's
denial of consequences as reasons for action.

Let us take an example of a maxim and see how Kant deals with it in
terms of the Categorical Imperative. By doing this we shall see his meaning

more clearly. Suppose I have promised that I will meet my friend Bill outside the cinema at eight o'clock. But at half-past seven I receive a telephone call inviting me to meet Donna at the disco. Bill is a good friend and I see him most evenings. However, Donna does not come to town very often and if I do not see her tonight, I shall not get the chance to see her again for a year. I am really very fond of Donna. Well, the utilitarian moralist would deal with this issue by reference to rules and possible consequences. Kant thinks differently. I have a genuine choice: I can tell Donna the truth that I have a previous engagement; or I can break my promise to Bill. (Let us suppose that Bill and the cinema are too far from Donna and the disco for me to keep both appointments. Moreover Bill is not on the telephone.)

My *desire* is to see Donna but my *duty*, according to Kant, is to keep my promise to Bill. Why? Because, says Kant, it is *always* my duty to keep my promises. This is where the utilitarian raises his eyebrows and starts to invent a few extreme cases which he thinks *prove* the fact that it is sometimes morally necessary to break one's promises. Kant will have none of this. He asks what would be the logical result if my maxim 'I shall break my promise' were to become a universal law. His answer is not that of a strong rule utilitarian who would argue that, as a matter of fact, the consequences for everyone would be simply dreadful if everyone obeyed a universal law in favour of breaking promises. Kant appeals to reason and logic. A law which proclaimed that promises should be broken turns out to be a nonsense purely and simply because it does away with all meaningful talk about promises. If no promise were *ever* kept, then the meaning of the word 'promise' would be denied. It would just mean that no one could ever talk about promises. A society which invented the practice of promising and then invented a rule that said all promises should be broken would by so doing merely contradict itself.

There is no doubt that Kant's doctrine of the Categorical Imperative indicates a simple and pure form of morality. There is great comfort in the words 'always' and 'never'. They provide us with security in moral matters because they help us to avoid all those oddly misleading cases which we discussed earlier. Moreover, we think we see something noble and good in Kant's point of view which, after all, gets rid of self-interest as a principle of action. And there is a strong anti-utilitarian streak in all of us. We suspect that a system of morality which allows us to wriggle out of obligations which we sometimes find inconvenient — as utilitarianism seems to allow us — is a rather less exalted business than the apparently pure doctrine of Immanuel Kant.

But it has been argued that Kant's doctrine of the Categorical Imperative contains just this kind of loophole. Kant says it would be inconsistent for me to universalise a maxim such as 'I may break my promises when I find it is convenient for me to do so.' But what if I were to make the maxim more specific? Remember, the *only* test prescribed by the Categorical

Imperative is that *any* maxim should be capable of being applied to everyone in the form of a law. Well suppose I were to invent the maxim, 'I may break my promises only when those promises are made to Bill and only when Donna has come up from the country.' This would allow me to meet Donna at the disco. But only if it is universalisable. Is it universalisable without contradiction? The answer would appear to be 'yes'. 'Everyone is allowed by law to break his promises only when those promises are made to Bill and only when Donna is up from the country.' As Alasdair MacIntyre says of this sort of subtlety: 'It follows that in practice the test of the Categorical Imperative imposes restrictions only on those insufficiently equipped with ingenuity. And this is scarcely what Kant intended.'

Not only is this not what Kant intended, it is also the utilitarian philosophers' severest criticism of all forms of ethics of the Kantian type. If *any* maxim can become a moral law simply because it can be universalised without logical inconsistency, then morality becomes divorced from the practicalities of day-to-day living. Moreover it could be so easily abused by an authoritarian regime. Take for instance, 'I ought to shoot all dissidents.' This becomes 'Everyone ought to shoot all dissidents.' Kant can only consistently uphold his universalisation principle — the Categorical Imperative — by agreeing that such a proposition about the fate of dissidents should also be upheld. After all, it involves no contradiction. But it is difficult to see the morality of such rash authoritarianism. Moral philosophers who disagree with Kant accuse him of inventing a doctrine which is capable of lending support to the most dictatorial regimes. Nor is this what Kant intended.

Bertrand Russell has argued that it is by no means obvious in every case which maxims are capable of universalisation. Kant says that 'Commit suicide' could never become a universal law. Russell says, 'It would be quite possible for a melancholic (an extremely sad and pessimistic person) to wish that everybody should commit suicide.' A melancholic may seriously and deeply believe that there is no good reason for living. According to Russell's view of the Categorical Imperative, it is entirely reasonable that such a belief should be universalised. If there really is no reason for living, then *we should all* be better off dead! It is worth mentioning that Bertrand Russell did not himself believe that we should all be better off dead. But it is also worth mentioning why Russell did not believe this: precisely because he was a utilitarian philosopher who believed that there is a consequence component to morality which ensures that it is removed from Kant's purely logical sphere.

Kant insists that duty and desire are always distinct. I should never do my duty because I desire to do so — not even if that desire is unselfish. If I am a kind-hearted and generous person by nature then there is, according to Kant, always a danger that I shall do my duty not because it is my duty but simply because that is what I most *enjoy* doing! Indeed, I cannot do my duty out of enjoyment any more than I can do it by accident. It might possibly occur — and as a matter of fact it does frequently occur — that what I desire turns out to be the same as what my duty dictates. But this is only a non-moral coincidence. Desirable consequences may indeed happen by accident, but my duty is always willed. I mentioned the purity and nobility of this doctrine; it removes morality from the 'messy' areas of calculation and compromise based on the desirability of certain consequences. But this is also the weakness of Kant's point of view. For it is a strange sort of morality which never takes account of what men desire and how we feel about certain actions. The world of pure logic is somewhat removed from the world of experience. Surely morality should have some connection with what actually happens as well as with the austere and logical prescription about what can be formally universalised.

Kant considers the logical consequences of a maxim about breaking one's promises, but he does not enquire about the actual social consequences. He does not ask why the activity of keeping promises arose in the first place. If it arose out of man's experience of the good consequences of promise-keeping, then the worlds of what is moral and what is desirable are linked together whether Kant likes it or not.

As we might expect from Kant's separation of desire and morality, of inclination and duty, of consequences and what is right, he has little to say on what other philosophers think are matters of fundamental moral importance. Consider for instance the maxim, 'I ought to have more than one wife' — that is, it is my duty (perhaps) to have more than one wife; it is not a case of desire! If, in the 1980s in Britain, I will that this should be universalised, then I am going against the law of the land which does not allow polygamy. It cannot be my duty to go against the law. But if I live in a country which does allow polygamy, then I do not go against the law. At different times then or in different places *the same* maxim is considered right and wrong. Which is *really* right then — monogamy or polygamy? It is contradictory to try to universalise *both* maxims in the same society at the same time. If the universalisation of one of these maxims is right, how do I tell which maxim is the right one? The utilitarian asks questions about the consequences of these maxims in their universalised forms. Are there enough women to go round — so that *every* man can have more than one wife? What do the women think about this arrangement? Is society in general more or less benefited by polygamy? — and so on.

Kant avoids some of the difficulties involved simply by extending his definition of 'everyone' in 'Everyone should have more than one wife' to encompass all rational men at all times and in all places. It is not logically contradictory for all men to have more than one wife, therefore it is a proposition capable of being universalised. Therefore, it could be my duty to have more than one wife.

The utilitarian — as well as the social anthropologist — wants to know which state (monogamy or polygamy) is really right, in the sense of its being more conducive to human happiness. Kant thinks that human happiness should not be allowed to cloud the issue. Happiness results from the satisfaction of desires and inclinations. For Kant the world of desires and inclinations is, as we have seen, quite distinct from the world of will, duty and moral obligation. In the end it is an odd system of morality which takes no account of practical consequences. In Oscar Wilde's words, it is as if Kant is saying, 'Nothing that actually happens is of the slightest importance.'

Another difficulty with Kant's moral philosophy arises out of the difference between moral propositions and non-moral ones. If I am not allowed to appeal to consequences as the justification of moral acts — an act is good or bad according to results — to what then may I appeal in order to know what a moral proposition is when I see one? It seems fairly obvious that keeping one's promises, not stealing, not telling lies and so on all have something to do with morality. The utilitarian explains why these actions are concerned with morality in terms of their consequences. For instance, 'Stealing causes unhappiness, so it is immoral to steal.' Kant appeals only to the logical thesis of universalisation.

Take the proposition, 'I ought to paint my walls green.' Is this a moral proposition or not? Kant replies that it is if it can be universalised without contradiction. It can be universalised. So it is a moral proposition. But this is absurd. The point remains, however, that unless we introduce some external principle like consequences or God's will, *any* proposition no matter how trivial can be called a moral principle purely on the grounds that it can be universalised without contradiction. We have seen Kant's opposition to the whole idea of consequences in moral theory. He is also against the importation of *any* other alleged guide to action such as the will of God. Leaving aside the theological question of how I can ever know what the will of God is, Kant argues that, if I do my duty because I believe it is God's will that I do it, then I am not acting purely morally. I am importing a concept irrelevant to morals. According to Kant, this is just as great an error in the case of what I allege to be God's will as it is in the case of what I believe will be good consequences. This mistaken acceptance of utilitarian or theological principles as a guide to morals is called by Kant 'heteronomy' — literally 'an other law' — and he says we should always avoid it. I wonder how devious your thinking is? What if we should try to universalise 'I ought to appeal to heteronomy in all moral dilemmas'? It does not seem to be contradictory unless we *first* accept Kant's view of morality — in which case it is of course clearly contradictory. But unless we accept Kant's view we have no reason to accept his opposition to heteronomy, for if we take an unprejudiced rational view we see that an appeal to heteronomy is not contradictory. So two opposing points of view can both be justified by Kant's philosophy and Kant is left with the unenviable task of trying to defend the outcome: a proposition which can be universalised in strict accordance with his doctrine of the Categorical Imperative is thrown out as entirely unacceptable.

Kant suggests that we can avoid the absurdity present in the doctrine that any universalisable proposition is a moral proposition by the further suggestion that moral propositions are immediately recognisable for what they are. In other words he assumes a general background of moral rules and theory. Unfortunately, as we saw in chapter one in the discussion of intuition, this is not as easy as it sounds. The moral world, noble and distinct above the world of inclination and desires, is not only quite divorced from how we actually live, it is also curiously difficult to identify.

I said that Kant does not think we can invoke the will of God in order to tell either what our duty is or why we should do our duty. But Kant is not an atheistic philosopher. He sees that virtue is not rewarded fully in this life; there is often undeserved suffering. So he says there must be God and an immortal life where the balance is redressed. The author and satirist, Heinrich Heine (1797-1856), said that Kant had developed this part of his ethics only to please the police. For Kant himself said that when men lost their respect for supernatural authority they would soon lose respect for the laws of society. Perhaps this was just an unfair jibe. But it seems odd to leave God out of your moral theory at its most important points only to bring God in to play a supporting role. Whatever Kant's actual beliefs about God — and we have no definite idea about these — he does seem to introduce the concept of God as an afterthought. It may be of course that there is no God, but that is not the point. On the other hand, *if* there is a God — and Kant says there is — then it seems strange to relegate the Supreme Being to the level of a verbal aside.

We have tried to analyse and criticise Kant's moral theory. I began by saying he was one of the greatest modern philosophers. If, after all this criticism, I were to try to say why I still stand by this judgement, it is because of Kant's attempt to show that morality is above what is petty and perishable. Whatever the difficulties that attend the working out of the doctrine of the Categorical Imperative, Kant showed that what defines human beings, what separates us from animals, is our morality and our ability to think about our morality rationally and independently of self-interest.

Things to think about and things to do

> If something is to be, or is held to be, absolutely <u>good</u> or <u>evil</u> in all respects and without qualification (which is essential to the moral concept of <u>the good</u>), it could not be a thing, but only a manner of acting, i.e. it could only be the <u>maxim</u> of the <u>will,</u> and consequently the acting person himself as a good or evil man. (from *The Critique of Practical Reason*).

*(1)   Look at the words underlined in the passage above and make sure
       you understand what they mean in the context of Kant's moral
       thought. Do you think he succeeded in showing that good and evil
       are not things in the world but qualities of the will?*
(2)   What is Kant's opinion about what is good?
(3)   What is the function of the good will?
(4)   Write down Kant's doctrine of the Categorical Imperative.
*(5)   Which acts does Kant regard as the sort of acts which it is unreasonable
       (because inconsistent) to perform?*
*(6)   Describe an argument between Kant and a utilitarian which starts with
       the utilitarian's statement, 'In some cases I am not sure what is my
       duty.'*
(7)   Are duty *and* desire *always distinct?*
(8)   Is the Principle of Universalisability the only *necessity for constructing
       moral arguments?*
(9)   Do the criticisms of intuitionism also apply to Kant?
*(10) Say in a couple of paragraphs whether you think Kant was a good
       moral philosopher.*

III Karl Marx (1818-1883)

It is impossible to leave Karl Marx out of a book which seeks to give a
general view of morality and which aims to present a picture of the
various ways in which societies have organised themselves. States that base
their system of government and social morality at least partly on what
Marx wrote include China (1000 million people), Russia (250 million),
Eastern Europe (190 million) and many emerging nations in Africa and
South America. In other words, half the world claims to organise its affairs
according to the precepts of Marxism.

Marxist or Communist philosophy is regarded with much suspicion and
disapproval in the countries of Western Europe and in the USA because
'capitalist', 'democratic' or 'free' countries tend to the view that Marxism
is a threat to their survival — or at least to the survival of particular
political systems. This suspicion is sometimes given an extreme
conspiratorial flavour and Marxist plots are alleged all over the place. You
are sure to have come across the expression 'Reds under the bed' or the
injunction 'Better dead than Red' — meaning that people of the Western
democracies should go to war rather than face Communist domination.
To understand the nature of this suspicion and of this threat we must
look at what Karl Marx really believed.

Marx began by looking at the industrial society of his own time, that
of the later phase of the industrial revolution. He believed that society
is shaped by the available technology and what he called 'the division of
labour'. Moreover, it is organised and geared up to make money. The
division of labour is unjust since a few (the employers) make a lot of

money while the many (the employed) are always paid less than they have actually earned according to what they have produced — Marx thought he had proved this conclusively by his theory of *surplus value* — the difference between the cost of a product measured by how much was paid to the worker and the amount for which the product is eventually sold. The unequal distribution of wealth gives rise to what Marx called 'class conflict' — the employers against the employed.

Marx saw that, however much was produced and however much profit was made, there was always an unfair distribution of wealth. If the worker receives an increase in wages it is only because the employer has granted himself an even greater increase. He said that there is no use for philanthropy — a generous and enlightened employer providing richly for his workers — because what is wrong is the whole structure of society into classes. No amount of philanthropy can remove the need for class conflict. Marx was an atheistic philosopher. He believed that man's freedom is restricted not by supernatural powers but by forces that are merely economic and that can therefore be changed.

If the workers are ever to receive justice and if their lot is to be genuinely improved, then the economic and social structures must be changed and a classless society must be created. Marx said that this would take a revolution before it could be achieved. 'The workers have nothing to lose but their chains. They have a world to gain. Workers of the world, unite!' Marx thought it was not only money and property of which the working class was deprived by the capitalist system operated in industrialised Europe; they were dehumanised by the appalling conditions in which they had to perform their labour. For an account of those conditions you might like to look at a book called *The Condition of the Working Class in England in 1844* by Marx's friend and collaborator, Friedrich Engels (1820-1895).

If you have read the early chapters of this book, you might now be asking on what moral theory did Marx base his revolutionary social ethics. It was obviously not divine revelation since he did not believe in God. In fact he regarded religion as an evil occupation because it provided false comfort for the working class and turned their thoughts away from the class struggle. 'Religion is the opium of the people.' Neither was Marx's system built on the principle of utility, the greatest happiness of the greatest number, because only the working class's interests will be served by his revolution. He was no existentialist. He was no Kantian.

To answer this question we must look briefly at Marx's theory of knowledge: what is it that men may rightly claim knowledge of and how is that knowledge obtained? Marx replied that knowledge derives from 'dialectical materialism'. By this puzzling phrase Marx meant to say that knowledge is not of anything static to which we might give the name 'matter'; nor is it of abstract ideas. Our knowledge comes through our relationship with objects and this relationship is called the dialectic. For

Marx there was no other genuine knowledge. This knowledge is not speculative. Marx said in the second of his *Eleven Theses on Feuerbach*, 'The dispute over the reality or non-reality of thinking which is isolated from practice is a purely scholastic question.' Also, 'Philosophers have only interpreted the world in various ways but the real task is to alter it.' Marx was in fact an example of Nietzsche's (1844-1900) ideal philosopher who does his thinking 'with a hammer'.

If it had not been for the doctrine of dialectical materialism, there would have seemed little difference between the thoughts of Karl Marx and those of any other radical who aimed for a dramatic improvement in the living standards of the poor and an attendant alteration in the structure of power. It was political and moral pressure from those radicals — some of them were Christians which might lead one to believe that religion was more of a stimulant than an opiate! — which brought about the famous Reform Acts of 1832 and 1867 and the abolition of slavery. And it is the doctrine of dialectical materialism which forces us to see Marx as something other than a pure reforming spirit. On this doctrine all the rest of Marx's moral and political thought depends. Let us examine it in detail.

First, if truth is located in man's relationship with objects, then it follows that, by acting in this way rather than that, one truth rather than another will be discovered. So far so good, but if truth is only a function, a result, of action, how can I know what it is *right* for me to do? For example, I might go to the orchestra practice or to the training session; whichever I do, one and only one description of my action will be correct. Either I went to the orchestra or else I went to the training session. But which *ought* I to have attended? If there are no abstract truths on which to base my judgement then from where do I derive my values? Marx was quite clear about this. He reckoned we must discover what we ought to do *only* in so far as that action aids the class struggle and helps promote the revolution. But if I ask why I should support the revolution there are only two answers according to Marx: first because he says I should; secondly because the revolution is inevitable. We shall come back to the second reason. Sufficient to comment here, 'Well, yes, and death is also inevitable but I do not on that account vote for it!'

Marx's defence of dialectical materialism by appealing to the intrinsic rightness of class warfare and revolution presents difficult problems. For if he cannot show that revolutionary morality is right by appeal to any rational principle, it would seem that there is no reason at all why anyone should agree with him out of anything other than self-interest. To be fair to Marx, he does admit that no one who does not belong to the oppressed working class has any reason to agree with him. In the absence of abstract truths and faced with the pointlessness of speculative philosophy of the type that Aristotle regarded as the highest good, all morality is class-based. There are no universal values. Many philosophers disagree with Marx here.

I believe that it is always wrong to torture the innocent without any other purpose than a hope that by so doing I will derive pleasure. Many other people will agree with me on this issue — people from all classes in society. This seems to me to prove that not all moral judgements are class-based. And if they are not class-based then they are derived according to some other principle. I suggest that this principle — whatever it might be, the will of God or the greatest happiness of the greatest number — has at least some connection with speculative thought of the kind which Marx regards as useless.

Besides, the denial of the value of speculative thought seems an odd stance for one like Marx to take — one who spent all those years in the British Museum poring over his books and papers and refining his doctrines. Actually, what Marx says is rather more subtle. He says that speculative reason is allowed so long as it is at the service of revolutionary aims. Unfortunately for Marx, rationality is not so partial nor so partisan. And if rationally, speculation and abstract ideas are all to be denied, what becomes of mathematics and the ordinary rules of logic? I am not the first person who has thought that Marx's doctrine of dialectical materialism and class-based philosophy implies the proposition that if the party says '2+3=6 is true', then it is true. If this seems absurd it is not my fault but Marx's fault. For it is Marx who denies the existence of abstract truths. Is '2+3=5' an abstract truth or is it only a matter of opinion? For Marx, all truth is subordinate to his revolutionary aims.

Secondly, if all truth is class-based, then it would appear that Marx's doctrines, if true, must also be class-based. We can then ask the question, 'But is what Marx says really true?' The reply that our question is meaningless seems unsatisfactory not to say gratuitously insulting; more seriously, it emphasises that everything which Marx ever meant by 'truth' and 'morality' is only a contentious opinion. Marx's moral statements are like slogans: 'Revolution is good for you' or 'Dialectical Materialism Rules OK.' That they *must* be slogans is not determined by unfair criticism of Marx, but by his own denial of the validity of speculative thought.

Indeed there is a logical method which makes plain Marx's 'mistake' about the nature of rational thought (or if not his mistake, at least his deliberate subordination of rational thought to political prejudice). This is a method which can be applied against all forms of irrationalism. No one who uses a language can deny the validity of rational thought for if he does, he defeats his own argument. This follows from the fact that all languages imply rules. To use a language means to accept the principle of rationality. It would be meaningless, and therefore self-defeating, to use a rational form such as language in order to deny rationality. This is an argument which can be advanced against all the many varieties of irrationalism whether these appear in moral philosophy or in the perplexing jargon of the fringe religious cults. When Marx and Engels admitted that the arguments of Berkeley (1685-1753) were 'hard to beat by mere argumentation', they gave away the clue to their own thinking: argumentation, logic and reason are regarded as qualities to which it is appropriate to apply the adjective 'mere'. Should we think *illogically* then? Marx's reply must be that indeed we must if by so doing we further the revolution. But to claim that in any circumstances anyone should choose to think illogically is merely to demonstrate that one has not understood the verb 'to think'.

Thirdly, there is Marx's doctrine of the inevitability of revolution. As we saw in the case of death, because something is inevitable that does not make it right. And Marx admits that the revolution will not seem right to anyone except members of one class. But leave aside the question of right for a moment and let us ask whether the revolution really is inevitable. Marx inherited the basis for this idea from the philosopher Hegel (1770-1831) who thought that the world of men and objects rearranged itself constantly under the influence of 'Spirit' which forever reinterprets itself in history. This was the original dialectic, and according to Hegel it can be compared with progression in music* from discord to concord, from tension to resolution. Maybe at the orchestra practice they play F # and G together, then resolve this discordance into the concord or consonance of the major triad C, E, G. For Hegel, and hence for Marx, history evolves first as 'thesis'; this is followed by a contradiction, 'antithesis', which is in turn resolved into 'synthesis'. The whole programme then begins again. You might be tempted to agree with Bertrand Russell's humorous criticism of Hegel — that the whole historical process consists in the eternally thwarted attempts of 'Spirit' to understand Hegel! What Marx did was to get rid of Hegel's mystical idea of 'Spirit' but then to take up his doctrine of the dialectic more or less intact. This is how he could claim that the revolution is 'inevitable'. But this claim, like other sayings in Marx's philosophy, is only a slogan, a bit of encouragement for those engaged in class warfare. Marx cannot prove that the revolution is 'inevitable' any more than evangelical Christians can prove that the Kingdom of God is 'coming soon'. Besides, 'soon' and 'inevitable' are words which share a convenient vagueness.

Fourthly, there are specific difficulties over that saying of Marx about the function of philosophy not being to understand the world but to change it. If we do not understand the world, how can we sensibly change it? The logical difficulty here is allied to Marx's practical reticence in telling us anything beyond a few generalities about either how the revolution is to be brought about or what life will be like after it. Certainly Marx thought it would be difficult to avoid some bloodshed but he said that the class war would be waged 'with concepts'. As we have seen, the concepts must first be well and truly baptised in the name of Marxist philosophy. It is for this vagueness that Marx is susceptible

---

* Actually, the idea is much older than this and in one form or another goes back to Pythagoras (sixth century BC) and the early Greek philosophers.

to strong criticism from the utilitarians. They would want to know exactly how any revolution should begin and according to what principles it should proceed. They would want to know also about the final outcome. Only on this information could a utilitarian decide whether any revolution would be a good thing or a bad thing. But for Marx all such questions are idle speculation. For him the revolution is its own justification and it is therefore beyond question and criticism. It is inevitable according to the only moral law that Marx will accept — the irresistible development of industrial society along the lines of his own philosophy. In this chapter we have at least questioned the two pillars upon which this philosophy stands: whether it is good and even whether it is inevitable. If Marx cannot show *reasons* for what he believes — reasons which go beyond his own highly personal characterisation of reason as a mere tool in the revolutionary struggle — then there are, on the face of it, grounds for asserting that if religion is the opium of the people, then Marxism is the opium of a certain class of political and moral theorists.

Fifthly, because of Marx's vagueness on these basic issues, the interpretations of his philosophy even by his own followers — *especially* by his own followers — are much at variance. And the moral disagreement is frequently greater among rival groups of Marxists than it is between them and the ruling class who they claim are the real enemies of the revolution. In the fourth century the Christian Church was divided into many different sects and groupings all of which claimed that they possessed a privileged insight into the truth. There were Arians, Appollinarians, Nestorians, Pelagians, Augustinians and so on. In the same way and in a much shorter time the same thing has happened to Marxism. There are literally hundreds of Marxist sects and parties, each of which claims that it alone faithfully represents the original purity of Marxist teaching. So in practical terms it is exceedingly difficult for the analyst and critic of contemporary Marxism to know what he is criticising. But just as all those early Christian sects used one set of terminology, 'Father', 'Son', 'Holy Spirit', 'Person', 'Substance', 'Incarnation' and so on, so the Marxist groupings do the same. The quarrel is over what any of them means by 'Revolution', 'Class', 'Consciousness', 'Dialectical Materialism' and the rest. We shall see that there are indeed similarities between the social morality of Marxism and the demands of religion.

Like the Christian convert, the revolutionary Marxist is urged to commit himself wholeheartedly. Just as the Christian may have to 'leave father and mother for my sake and the Kingdom' so the Marxist must give himself completely to the cause. Class warfare might be described as the Marxist equivalent of the Christian demand that believers should separate themselves from unbelievers and unrighteousness. Marx himself is regarded as a prophet and more than a prophet by his followers. He is a messianic figure and in this he fulfils the role in Marxism filled in Christianity by Jesus Christ. The Revolution is a secularised form of the Last Judgement.

And the Classless Society which is supposed to come after the revolution compares with the Kingdom of Heaven. Marxists and Christians find these parallels odious but there is no denying that the underlying *structures* of both systems are very similar. (Russell draws even closer attention to these similarities in his book *History of Western Philosophy* p.361, 1961 edition.)

Perhaps in this comparison we glimpse something of the essence of Marxism when we consider it as a kind of religion which attracts, fascinates and inspires rather than as a philosophy which seeks to persuade by rational argument. There is something of the style of the Old Testament prophet in Marx (see the Book of Amos) as he denounces injustice and proclaims the inevitable dawn of a new age of righteousness once the evil has been purged. And who is to say that such a call to conversion (revolution) was not needed amid the horrors of nineteenth-century industrial society? The fact is, of course, that Marx was not alone in indicating the problems; only his system with all its romance and its once-and-for-all commitment to an ideal proved to be more attractive than the more mundane utilitarian calculus employed by some of the radicals of the time.

The work of the non-Marxist reformers has, of course, been hampered by sectional interest and selfishness. This is what Marx was against just as the Old Testament prophet was against sin. A question to be considered in the face of all these good intentions is whether doctrinal purity and good intentions alone constitute sufficient reason for drawing up a philosophy of social morality which is incoherent and unconvincing because finally irrational.

Another question might be couched in the light of experience. In which nations has the working-class achieved most freedom and other benefits — in those nations which claim to follow Marx's doctrines or in others which do not? There are those who think that post-war events in Hungary, Czechoslovakia and Poland (as well as in Mao's Cultural Revolution) say much of what needs to be said on that matter. It might be claimed — and indeed it is sometimes claimed — that as a matter of fact no modern Communist state has faithfully put into practice Marxist doctrines. Even if this were true, the fact would remain that Marxism allows for *any* means for its own spread throughout the world — the revolution and the world-wide Marxist Commonwealth are regarded as justification for any methods. This includes the method of resisting and even denying the validity of opponents' rational arguments if these arguments are against Marxist dogma. That such methods are used by certain modern states which call themselves Marxist cannot be denied. Also, that this method of riding rough-shod over logic and rational criticism stands against all genuinely philosophical interests goes without saying.

Things to think about and things to do

The philosophers have only interpreted the world in various ways; the point however is to change it. (from *Eleven Theses on Feuerbach*)

(1)   Read the quotation above. How does Marx describe the processes of interpretation and revolution? Is it possible to change anything before one has interpreted it?

(2)   Why does Marx think that 'class war' is unavoidable?

(3)   What is meant by 'dialectical materialism'?

(4)   Why should anyone support the revolution? Is Marx's answer to this question convincing?

(5)   Is the revolution 'inevitable'?

(6)   How can we 'change' the world unless we first 'understand' what we aim to change? Is Marx's philosophy irrational?

(7)   'If the Party says 7+5=11 then they are right. That's the sort of nonsense that puts me off Marxism!' Has this caricature any truth in it?

(8)   Make a list of the similarities between Marxism and Christian doctrine as described in this chapter. Was Marx a secularised prophet?

7 Conclusion – the possibility of morals

There are two very common attitudes to philosophy in general and to moral philosophy in particular: the first regards it as an interesting mental exercise; the second regards it as a form of tedious talk in which simple truths are rendered difficult and plain things are made obscure. Neither of these two attitudes values philosophy as an activity which is actually *useful*. Both attitudes draw a sharp distinction between *thinking* and *doing*. And even people who find philosophy can be fun do not always think that it is of any practical value. After all, what difference does it make? The world will still go on no matter what you or I may think!

It is easy to have sympathy with this conclusion. Philosophy seems to have little connection with everyday life. We are not regularly called upon to make far-reaching moral decisions about such sensational issues as test-tube babies, nor to juggle with the ethical conundrums of that Captain in *The Cruel Sea*. As we noticed at the beginning of the book, we do not ordinarily think very much about moral issues for most of the time. What then is the use of moral philosophy?

I suggest that thinking about morality has two main functions apart from the enjoyment and good clean fun which may be derived from this exercise. First, it is a means by which we can rationally examine any new thing in the sphere of private or public life — whether a proposed new law of the land is a good law or whether a technological innovation (like transplant surgery) should be welcomed or resisted. Secondly, reasoning about morality is the only non-violent way of settling disagreements about how human beings should behave. But there is another and even more important reason for doing moral philosophy. We do go about our lives for the most part without thinking very much about the reasoning which goes into the formulation of morality. But we are able to do this, to be generally unreflecting on our behaviour only because we *have learned how to behave*. I meet you in the street and we agree to meet again later outside the cinema. Neither of us goes away from that first meeting and agonises all day about whether to keep the second date. We do not spend the whole day puzzling over whether morality obliges us always to keep our promises. We do keep our promises nonetheless. In the same way, hardly anyone feels compelled to repeat under his breath all the moral arguments against stealing every time he stands outside a jeweller's window. But the reason why he does not have to do this is because serious thinking about theft and moral rules has taken place already and definite conclusions have been established. There is a rule about stealing which for the most part goes unquestioned. Had that moral thinking which led to the rule not taken place, then there would have been no rule. The result: chaos.

There is a simple parallel of moral reasoning with practical reasoning. For example, we do not give much thought to the Law of Gravity as we go about our daily business. The law operates just the same. Similarly, we do not concern ourselves much with the foundations of moral knowledge but we still behave morally every day of our lives. We take physical laws like the Law of Gravity and moral rules like the prohibition of stealing for granted. We should not forget that both sorts of laws were actually thought out at some time in the past and that our physical and moral well-being depends on the fact that some people did take the trouble to do the original thinking. For the most part we are able to take moral philosophy for granted simply because our predecessors did not. All those 'rules of thumb' – not stealing, not telling lies but keeping promises and so on – were once worked out and reasons were given for their general acceptance.

It has been claimed that moral philosophy is constructed out of extreme cases. This is true. Moral arguments begin when an existing moral rule is challenged. Take, for example, the new ability to prolong life which has come with transplant surgery. There is no longer any doubt that in certain circumstances life *can* be prolonged; the moral argument arises out of whether it *ought* to be prolonged. The old medical ethics seem to speak uncertainly on this issue and so new insights and new moral arguments are brought to bear upon it. Eventually a code of practice is established. This code of practice represents general agreement on the moral issue of, say, heart transplants. For instance, should men aged between thirty and forty-five, married and with children take precedence over unmarried women in their sixties when it comes to deciding how the available transplant technology shall be made available. This is an example of moral philosophy in the market place; rules for conduct and practice being hammered out in the light of experience.

Of course, not everyone will accept any new moral rule or code of practice. Here we see the importance of moral philosophy for providing a means of reasonable discussion and dissent. In the case of a law about the compulsory wearing of seat-belts in cars, one person might say simply, 'Well, I don't like that law.' Unless he can give reasons for his disapproval and disagreement we shall not take much notice of his protests. Objections which do not have rational backing will tend to be regarded as mere matters of taste. 'I do not like the new law' will have no more power to influence our beliefs than 'I do not like marshmallows'. Once reasons are advanced, the issue is of concern to moral philosophers and to anyone who looks for a rational basis for conduct in society. In the case of compulsory wearing of seat-belts for instance, one person will oppose the law on the grounds that it is an infringement on human freedom; a man ought to be free not to wear a seat-belt so long as he is prepared to face the consequent risk to his life. Another person will reply that the number of lives that would be saved by a law compelling the wearing of seat-belts is a consideration which far outweighs the consideration of human freedom in this case.

The objector will protest that a man ought to be free to kill himself, or at least to run the greater risk of killing himself that comes from not wearing a seat-belt. But the supporter of the law might reply that it is not simply a case of one man or even of all drivers being free to kill themselves if that is what they are prepared to risk; it is also the case that seat-belts protect passengers, that they reduce the risk of injury to everyone involved in car accidents, that they help to make people more safety-conscious on the roads, that by reducing the number of accidents they also reduce the claims made upon medical resources and so on.

You might like to consider the argument that there ought to be a law which bans the smoking of cigarettes on similar grounds. The argument will be joined by supporters of a variety of moral standpoints: the person who claims that freedom to smoke is a natural right which must not be removed; the person who claims, on utilitarian grounds, that since the consequences of smoking are so bad, all considerations of natural rights should not be allowed to interfere. Both the supporter of natural rights and *another* utilitarian might reply by saying that, if individual freedom is denied by a law which bans smoking, then we have no guarantee that freedom will continue to be respected in other areas of life. You might try to get this argument going among a group of your friends and examine the moral standpoints involved, see how they relate to the various moral theories put forward in our earlier chapters. Just for fun:

Supporters of Natural Law:	Tobacco exists therefore it is right to smoke.
Act Utilitarian:	I shall stop smoking because it makes me cough.
Rule Utilitarian:	Banning smoking may have good consequences *immediately* because it will reduce deaths from heart disease but it will encourage governments to think that they can do anything which they find convenient and this will lead to bad consequences *eventually*. So I am against the ban.
Existentialist:	I will smoke or not smoke as I choose. It is my own decision and that is all that I need to take into consideration.

Marxist: I support the ban. It will lead to even greater dissatisfaction with the government and so hasten the revolution.

What might Aristotle have said? What about Immanuel Kant? These are only examples of what a *particular* utilitarian, a *particular* Marxist, etc. might argue. Any or all of the examples I have given might have been quite different. For instance, the Marxist might have argued instead, 'I am against the ban. If people are allowed to smoke they are less tense and more efficient when they are fighting the revolution.' The point is that supporters of each point of view will give reasons for their opinions. The working out of these reasons is the function of moral philosophy.

It is also moral philosophy which allows for the possibility of moral disagreement and dissent. Human beings are not infallible and so it is rarely possible to say of any moral rule that it is always and absolutely right in all cases of its application. For example, most people would agree that it is usually right to try to prolong life. But sometimes it is thought desirable and morally good not to do so. For instance, in the case of a very old blind and deaf lady whose life is being lived out in terrible pain and who has expressed a wish that, if ever she should find herself in the condition in which she does now in fact find herself, then she should be allowed to die.

A reasonable society with a rule-utilitarian type system of morality will have to find a policy, a code of practice, which is to be operated in cases like that of the sick old lady. In fact, our society has already done so. It draws a distinction between actually killing off old patients and, in extreme cases of this kind, 'not strenuously striving to keep them alive'. Many members of our society disagree with this official policy. Some argue that euthanasia should be allowed in certain cases. Others argue that the present policy already goes too far towards euthanasia. The point is, once again, that all parties to the debate suggest *reasons* in support of their arguments. And society itself, while having adopted a particular policy, tolerates rational dissent from that policy. The important stipulation is that the dissent should be rational; anyone who objects to society's policy on this or other issues will be asked the reasons for his dissent. Anyone who dissents but who is not prepared to give reasons is called a fanatic.

Rational disagreements in matters of morals is one way in which changes and perhaps even progress in morals is achieved. Acceptable compromises are the prized results of weak rule utilitarianism. They are the basis on which society is able to change its mind and to face new problems as they arise. So in the end moral philosophy has very immediate and practical connections with the way we live. So far, however, we have only said that it is important for individuals to agree or to disagree rationally about moral issues. We have not drawn attention to any *particular* issue and asked questions about its rightness. This is at least partly because there is *so much* room for rational disagreement that it is difficult to say of any moral rule that it must be the right one.

But are there any moral rules which are so clear that no one can doubt their rightness? I believe that there are such rules but that they are few in number. They are the sorts of rules without which it would be impossible to imagine the existence of a society of *any sort*. Moreover, these are general principles rather than moral particulars. Why must they be general principles? Because particulars, being particulars, are concerned only with a tiny aspect of life while general principles, being general principles cover the whole of life. For example, a clear but particular moral rule such as 'Always wear your seat-belt in the car' could never be held to be a rule of universal necessity. This is because it is possible to imagine a society which does not have cars. Also because, although it would usually be considered a bad thing for ten thousand people to die annually in car crashes because they did not wear their seat-belts, it is still possible to imagine a society in which this great misfortune does happen.

In the case of general principles the results are quite different. It is impossible to imagine an ordered society in which no one takes any notice of the rule, 'Keep your promises' or the other rule, 'Do not steal'. You can perhaps detect echoes of Kant here. A society without rules about promises and theft would collapse into murderous chaos. Murder is another act that must be universally condemned. Philosophers go so far as to define 'murder' as wrongful killing; so it is immediately obvious to everyone that murder is wrong. 'Murder' means something that is wrong. Notice I have not said that all acts of killing are equally wrong. Some societies, like our own, grade acts of killing on a scale that runs from 'unprovoked malice' to 'patriotic duty'. To walk into a child's bedroom and cut his head off is a clear case of the first extreme; to defend Her Majesty against a vicious and wicked enemy is considered by many to be a clear case of the other extreme. There are, of course, many gradations in between for which we might use expressions like 'diminished responsibility' and 'mitigating circumstances'. While there will be disagreement about which acts of killing should be called 'murder', there can be no disagreement about murder itself as something that is always wrong. This is true simply because 'murder' is defined as a wrongful act. Killing may sometimes be right but murder is always wrong.

Something similar applies in the cases of keeping promises and not stealing. While there may be exceptional circumstances in which it might be right to break a promise or even to steal, no one but a fanatic could make 'Always break your promises' or 'Steal!' into a moral principle. Rules which state that we should keep our promises and refrain from stealing are sometimes said to be *constitutive* of human society. This means simply that no society could exist without them. Particular societies may differ as to particular rules but all societies agree on certain basic general principles such as the ones we have just mentioned.

If there is agreement on moral matters this is where it is to be found, in generalities. The real task of moral philosophy is that of applying general principles to particular cases and here, as we have seen, the range of reasonable opinions is very wide.

Perhaps you will agree that in a free society this is as it ought to be − if you see what I mean by 'ought'!

Things to think about and things to do
(1)   Why do we not need to spend nearly all our time worrying about how to make up our minds on moral issues?
(2)   Give an example of the sort of 'extreme case' which helps us to work out new moral principles.
(3)   What is the place of reason in morality?
(4)   Should I obey a law because it is a law or should I question all laws in order to discover whether they are good or not?
(5)   How does moral philosophy allow for moral disagreement?
(6)   Write down five points of view representing different moral philosophies about the problem of corporal punishment in schools. (One sentence each, of the 'I think . . . because . . .' type).
(7)   What sorts of moral rules have been held to be 'constitutive of morality'? Would you add other moral rules to this list?
(8)   How is an ordered society able to tolerate differences of opinion among its citizens on moral matters?

Further reading

1 General introduction to philosophy

Hospers, John *An Introduction to Philosophical Analysis*, RKP
Emmet, E.R. *Learning to Philosophise*, Penguin
Russell, B. *The Problems of Philosophy*, OUP paperback
Mullen, Peter *Beginning Philosophy*, Edward Arnold
Stebbing, L. Susan *Thinking to Some Purpose*, Pelican

2 Historical surveys of philosophy

Russell, B. *History of Western Philosophy*, George Allen and Unwin
Passmore, J. *A Hundred Years of Philosophy*, Pelican

3 Introductions to moral philosophy

Hospers, John *Human Conduct*, RKP
MacIntyre, Alasdair *A Short History of Ethics*, RKP

Chapter 1

Russell, B. *An Inquiry into Meaning and Truth*, Pelican
Ogden, C.K. and Richards, I.A. *The Meaning of Meaning*, RKP
Robinson, R. *Definition*, OUP
Ayer, A.J. *Language, Truth and Logic*, Pelican
Stevenson, C.L. *Ethics and Language*, Yale
Moore, G.E. *Ethics*, OUP
Hudson, W. *Ethical Intuitionism*, Papermac
Prichard, H.A. *Moral Obligation*, OUP

Chapter 2

MacGregor, G. *An Introduction to Religious Philosophy*, Macmillan
Hick, J. *Evil and the God of Love*, Fontana
St. Augustine *The Confessions of St. Augustine*, Fontana
Bouquet, A.C. *Comparative Religion*, Pelican
The Holy Bible, Cambridge, the King James version
O'Malley, C.L. *Popular Hinduism*, Cambridge

Bell, Richard *The Koran in English*, T. & T. Clark
Guillaume, A. *Islam*, Pelican
Arnold, Matthew *Literature and Dogma*, Nelson
Barr, J. *Fundamentalism*, SCM
Mullen, Peter *Thinking About Religion*, Edward Arnold

Chapter 3

O'Connor, D.J. *Aquinas and Natural Law*, Papermac
Anscombe, G.E.L. and Geach, P.T. *Three Philosophers*, Oxford
D'Entrèves, A.P. *Natural Law*, London

Chapter 4

Bowring, J. (ed.) *The Works of Jeremy Bentham*, London
Mill, J.S. *Utilitarianism*, Fontana
Fletcher, Joseph *Situation Ethics*, SCM
Hare, R.M. *Language of Morals*, Oxford
Hare, R.M. *Freedom and Reason*, Oxford
Toulmin, S. *An Examination of the Place of Reason in Ethics*, Cambridge

Chapter 5

Murdoch, Iris *Sartre*, Bowes and Bowes
Sartre, J.P. *Being and Nothingness*, Methuen
Sartre, J.P. *The Roads to Freedom* (3 vols.), Penguin
Sartre, J.P. *Nausea*, Penguin
Camus, A. *The Fall*, Penguin
Camus, A. *The Outsider*, Penguin
Camus, A. *The Plague*, Penguin
Camus, Λ. *The Rebel*, Penguin Modern Classics
Camus, A. *The Myth of Sisyphus*, Penguin
Warnock, Mary *Ethics since 1900*, Oxford
Warnock, Mary *Existentialist Ethics*, Oxford
Kierkegaard, S. *Either Or*, Princeton
Nietzsche, F. *Thus Spoke Zarathustra*, Penguin
MacQuarrie, J. *An Existentialist Theology*, SCM
Buber, M. *I and Thou*, Fontana
Tillich, P. *The Courage to Be*, Fontana
Bonhoeffer, D. *Letters and Papers from Prison*, Fontana

Chapter 6

Aristotle *Ethics*, Penguin Classics
Adkins, A.W.H. *Merit and Responsibility*, Clarendon

Kant, I. *Foundations of the Metaphysics of Morals*, Liberal Arts
Körner, S. *Kant*, Pelican
Wolff, R.P. (ed.) *Kant*, Papermac
Paton, H.J. *The Categorical Imperative*, London
Aiken, H.D. *The Age of Ideology*, Mentor
Burns, Emil (ed.) *A Handbook of Marxism*, Gollancz
McLellan, D. *Marx*, Fontana

Chapter 7

Mackie, J.L. *Ethics — Inventing Right and Wrong*, Pelican
Foot, Philippa *Theories of Ethics*, Oxford